T0151800

# THE GOSPEL OF GOD'S REIGN

Christoph Friedrich Blumhardt (1842–1919)

# The Blumhardt Source Series

Christian T. Collins Winn and Charles E. Moore, editors

# The Gospel of God's Reign

## *Living for the Kingdom of God*

### Christoph Friedrich Blumhardt

*Originally Selected and Arranged by* Eugen Jäckh

*Edited by* Christian T. Collins Winn
and Charles E. Moore

*Translated by* Peter Rutherford,
Eileen Robertshaw, and Miriam Mathis

PLOUGH PUBLISHING HOUSE

Published by Plough Publishing House
Walden, New York
Robertsbridge, England
Elsmore, Australia
www.plough.com

Translated from Christoph Blumhardt, *Vom Reich Gottes* (Schlüchtern: Neuwerk-Verlag, 1922) and *Von der Nachfolge Jesu Christi* (Berlin: Furche-Verlag, 1923).

ISBN: 978-0-87486-243-0
23 22 21 20 19   1 2 3 4 5 6 7 8

A catalog record for this book is available from the British Library.
Library of Congress Cataloging-in-Publication Data

Names: Blumhardt, Christoph, 1842-1919, author. | Collins Winn, Christian
 T., editor. | Moore, Charles E., 1956-, editor.
Title: The gospel of God's reign : living for the kingdom of God /
 Christoph Friedrich Blumhardt ; originally selected and arranged by
 Eugen Jäckh ; edited by Christian T. Collins Winn and Charles E. Moore
 ; translated by Peter Rutherford, Eileen Robertshaw, and Miriam Mathis.
Description: Walden NY : Plough Publishing House, 2019. | Series: Blumhardt
 series | Originally published: 2014.
Identifiers: LCCN 2019019179 | ISBN 9780874862430 (pbk.)
Subjects: LCSH: Kingdom of God--Sermons. | Christian life--Sermons. |
 Lutheran Church--Sermons. | Sermons, German--Translations into English.
 | Devotional literature, German.
Classification: LCC BT94.B62 A25 2019 | DDC 231.7/2--dc23
LC record available at https://lccn.loc.gov/2019019179

Dedicated to Eberhard Arnold (1883–1935)

*Humble witness to the coming future of God*
*Matthew 7:21–23*

# Contents

Series Foreword by Christian T. Collins Winn and Charles E. Moore · *xi*

Foreword by Nathan R. Kerr · *xiii*

Acknowledgments · *xvii*

Introduction by Christian T. Collins Winn · *xix*

1 God's Love · 1

2 The Reign of God · 14

3 The Living Christ · 29

4 Our Savior King · 51

5 God's People · 58

6 The Way of the Cross · 76

7 Hope and Expectation · 96

Introduction to the 1922 German Edition by Eugen Jäckh · 119

Scripture Index · 127

# Series Foreword

THE BLUMHARDT SOURCE SERIES seeks to make available for the first time in English the extensive oeuvre of Johann Christoph Blumhardt (1805–1880) and his son Christoph Friedrich Blumhardt (1842–1919), two influential religious figures of the latter half of the nineteenth century who are not well known outside their native Germany. Their influence can be detected in a number of important developments in nineteenth- and twentieth-century Protestantism: the recovery of the eschatological dimension of Christianity and the kingdom of God; the recovery of an emphasis on holistic notions of spirituality and salvation; the rise of faith healing and later, Pentecostalism; the convergence of socialism and the Christian faith; and the development of personalist models of pastoral counseling.

Their collected works make available their vast body of work to scholars, pastors, and laypeople alike with the aim of giving the Blumhardts a full hearing in the English language for the first time. Given the extent of their influence during the theological and religious ferment of the late nineteenth and early twentieth centuries, we believe that these sources will be of great interest to scholars of that period across various disciplines. It is also true, however, that there is much spiritual and theological value in the witness of the Blumhardts. We hope that by making their witness more widely known in the English-speaking world the church at large will benefit.

The project outline is flexible, allowing for volumes that aim either in a scholarly direction or towards the thoughtful lay reader. The emphasis will be to reproduce, with only slight modifications, the various German editions of the Blumhardts' works that have appeared since the late nineteenth century. A modest scholarly apparatus will provide contextual and theologically helpful comments and commentary through introductions, footnotes, and appendices.

During their long ministries, the elder and younger Blumhardt found themselves called to serve as pastors, counselors, biblical interpreters, theologians, and even politicians. No matter the vocational context, however, both understood themselves as witnesses to the kingdom of God that was both already present in the world, and also breaking into the current structures of the world. Together they represent one of the most powerful instances of the convergence of spirituality and social witness in the history of the Christian church. As series editors, it is our conviction that their witness continues to be relevant for the church and society today. We hope that the current series will give the Blumhardts a broader hearing in the English-speaking world.

Christian T. Collins Winn and Charles E. Moore

# Foreword

*Nathan R. Kerr*

THOUGH HE IS PERHAPS best known to the English-speaking world for the critical influence his life and thought had upon the practical formation of the Bruderhof movement, Blumhardt's scholarly—that is, "academic"—renown has mostly turned on the influence his thought has had upon such theological luminaries as Karl Barth, Dietrich Bonhoeffer, and Emil Brunner. His uncanny awareness of the "paradox" of the gospel has ensured his place alongside Kierkegaard and Overbeck as one of the forerunners of the "dialectical" school that emerged in the wake of Barth's second *Epistle to the Romans*, and that determined the course of so much of twentieth-century theology. Even today, Blumhardt has been heralded as the great-grandfather of a particular mode of "apocalyptic" thought that has emerged in contemporary theology. Such academic interpretations ensure for us that Blumhardt really does have something important to say as a theologian. But by prescribing in advance a particular method or theory for reading Blumhardt, such can equally serve to forestall any possibility that some wayward "lay" reader might stumble upon a book like this and find within it intimations to a way of living and working that cannot be so theorized.

That Christoph Blumhardt lived and worked and wrote in such a way as to resist the kind of theoretical capture that reduces theology to a mere intellectual peddling of the gospel is too often not only forgotten but deliberately ignored. The conveniences of *academe* do not allow for the appalling possibility that God might act in ways entirely unintelligible to human reason, much less that God might act so as to free us to live as silent, but active witnesses to that unintelligibility. And yet, if the gospel is a *power* that is to be experienced and lived, and not simply a *message* that is to be conceptualized and understood, as Blumhardt insists, we must admit that God might not only act against our own reason and expectations, but that faith in this God itself eschews understanding. "God has to be experienced. And whoever experiences him becomes speechless." Any gospel that does not test to destruction our own human theories or ideologies, as well as the so-called "religious" customs and institutions that perpetuate them in the name of "Christianity," is not the gospel of God's kingdom in which Jesus Christ *alone* reigns as Lord.

In *The Gospel of God's Reign* Blumhardt is not simply a pietistic thinker painfully groping his way toward various theological insights that came to be developed in the later "dialectical" theology and that are thoroughly theorized in contemporary "apocalyptic" thought. No, Blumhardt is speaking out of the conviction that true faith is born of the boundless love of God, not simply of theology and its various points of doctrine. As Blumhardt put it: "This is the gospel, 'You are loved.'" Furthermore, insofar as the love of God is not a *thing*, but a *way* lived out in the person of Jesus Christ, so faith itself is a living out of this love: "To believe in Jesus, means to love." No theological system can evoke this faith from us. Instead, this faith is a living response to the love of God in Christ whose work is precisely to deliver us from all false masters and human spheres of domination, by freeing us to love in the way of the cross.

Such faith comes to us only as God's love in Christ brings about a new creation, which breaks into this world in such a way as to bring to naught the powers and principalities that hold us in bondage and decay. "When God's love speaks, the world is made new. In Jesus Christ it will again be made new." In Christ, everything about this sinful and dying world is judged and condemned, so that everything about this sinful and dying world might be forgiven and brought to new life. It is for this reason that faith in Jesus Christ is for Blumhardt faith in the resurrection. Only from within the event of the resurrection is it possible to proclaim that "Jesus is victor!" while also praying "Thy Kingdom Come!" Only from within the event of resurrection is it possible to acknowledge that human life is in contradiction—sinful and fallen under the conditions of this old age, yet free for the coming new creation. That is to say, only from within the event of the resurrection is it possible to speak at once dialectically and apocalyptically without submitting the gospel to either a dialectical *method* or an apocalyptic *theory*.

For in the end, what matters for Christoph Blumhardt is that the resurrection of Jesus Christ is a reality here and now—that we experience its transforming power in the hope of Christ's coming in glory, and then give ourselves to it by working and fighting to resist the ways in which the powers of this world continue to imprison, oppress, and marginalize those very persons whom God's love in Christ has set free. As such, *The Gospel of God's Reign* is not fundamentally a work of theology—not because Blumhardt doesn't speak theologically, but because for Blumhardt the work of theology is to do nothing more and nothing less than to witness to the kind of existence facing the reader who would venture to live out this gospel in faith. The apocalyptic and even dialectical character of the gospel will not admit of any verification other than a life lived under the rule and reign of God, which means precisely in the life of that one reader who finds him or herself called to faith by the love of that God that is indeed witnessed to here in this text.

# Acknowledgments

THE EDITORS ARE INDEBTED to the Bruderhof Historical Archive, Walden, New York, USA, for providing original translated material, to Miriam Mathis for her painstaking work in translating and copyediting, to Jakob Gneiting for his ongoing commitment to keeping the witness of the Blumhardts alive, and to Dieter Ising and Ralf Breslau for their archival assistance.

# Introduction

*Christian T. Collins Winn*

## BLUMHARDT'S LIFE

CHRISTOPH FRIEDRICH BLUMHARDT (1842–1919) has been called many things: pastor, prophet, politician, theologian, socialist, and faith-healer to name but a few, though he would have understood himself as simply a witness to the kingdom of God. Often called "Blumhardt the Younger," Christoph Friedrich Blumhardt was born on June 1, 1842, to Johann Christoph (1805–1880) and Doris née Köllner Blumhardt (1816–1886) in the small village of Möttlingen just outside of Stuttgart. He was the third of eight children, though three of his siblings died in childbirth or at a very young age. Though Blumhardt was born in a typical farming village in Württemberg, it was during the most remarkable chapter of Möttlingen's history. In 1841, a local villager, Gottliebin Dittus, approached Johann Christoph Blumhardt, or "Blumhardt the Elder," complaining of "spiritual struggles," which she was experiencing especially at night. Initially repelled by Dittus, the elder Blumhardt would eventually find himself drawn into a conflict that lasted almost two years, and that he became convinced was a case of demonic possession. The dramatic dénouement and crescendo of the episode occurred in December of 1843, when the demonic power purportedly shrieked "Jesus is the victor!" which Blumhardt later came to understand was a confession made in the presence of the living Christ, who had come to do battle with the nefarious power. These remarkable and sensational events were followed by a regional revival, which lasted on and off for most of 1844.[1]

Though Christoph Blumhardt was but a small child, these events and the subsequent ministry of Blumhardt's father at Bad Boll constitute the imaginative and symbolic structure of the younger Blumhardt's theological world. Christoph grew up with the stories and personalities that had played a major role in the events at Möttlingen and was heir to the faith that those events had kindled. That faith, as expressed especially by the elder Blumhardt and summed up in the phrase "Jesus is the victor!" centered on the conviction that the kingdom of God, identified with the person of Jesus and the ministry of the Spirit, was a dynamic and living power that broke into history to set humanity free from spiritual and physical bondage. Under the influence of the eschatologically oriented Pietism of Württemberg, the elder Blumhardt articulated a vision of hope that had a chiliastic orientation—a hope for God's kingdom to be manifest in history and on the earth—though it was not captive to the temptation to develop timetables for the final return of Christ. Rather, Blumhardt's hope was focused especially on the "signs" of the kingdom's coming. That is, the elder Blumhardt was especially interested in how the small, ephemeral, and seemingly inconsequential moments of liberation that individuals and communities experienced were related to the definitive event of liberation described in Scripture as the "Day of the Lord."

For the elder Blumhardt, though the penultimate events of liberation and salvation were not to be confused with the final arrival of God's kingdom, they were nonetheless demonstrative signs or pointers. These, in turn, kindled hope and were intended to structure the life of discipleship such that the basic orientation of the Christian was "active prayer" for the coming kingdom, the final in-breaking of God's reign in which all things would be made right. "Active prayer" referred to the struggle that Christians were called to engage in on behalf of the coming kingdom. So, even though God brings both "signs of the kingdom" as well as the kingdom itself, the Christian community was called to struggle alongside God for the coming of God's kingdom. This struggle manifested itself not only in seeking healing through prayer, fasting, and worship, but also in and through active service,

---

1. See Dieter Ising, *Johann Christoph Blumhardt, Life and Work: A New Biography* (Eugene, OR: Cascade, 2009) 140–227; and Friedrich Zündel, *Pastor Johann Christoph Blumhardt: An Account of His Life*, Blumhardt Series (Eugene, OR: Cascade, 2010) 117–297. See also Johann Christoph Blumhardt, *Blumhardt's Battle: A Conflict with Satan* (New York: Lowe, 1970).

works of mercy, and justice. All of these were tangible forms of witness to the coming kingdom, concrete enactments of the second petition of the Lord's Prayer: "Thy kingdom come!"[2]

This was the faith and faith-community in which Christoph Blumhardt was nurtured. Although he studied theology at Tübingen from 1862 to 1866, the greatest influence on him was undoubtedly his father and the spiritual community of Bad Boll.[3] Christoph, however, did not simply repeat his father's thought and ministry. After his father's death in 1880, he took over as spiritual leader of the community at Bad Boll. But in the late 1880s, coinciding with the death of the last participants in the Möttlingen "Kampf," Blumhardt began to undergo a profound change.

The passing of the Möttlingen generation led Blumhardt to consider the ephemeral nature of the Möttlingen experience itself. Rather than it representing the last, penultimate sign of God's in-breaking—which he felt was his father's position—it too was but a weigh-station. What was needed was a retooling to discern where and how God was now at work in history. This reconsideration led Blumhardt to conclude that the kingdom of God was breaking into the world in new and different ways and in particular in the cry for social justice coming out of the Workers' Movement taking place throughout Europe in the latter half of the nineteenth and first part of the twentieth century. For the elder Blumhardt, "Jesus is the victor!" included the *healing of the body*; for Christoph it now included the *healing of the body politic*. Thus Christoph began to envision the struggle for God's kingdom as a fight with the powers and principalities that were embedded in social and political structures. As Eugen Jäckh notes in the original introduction to the present work, the most decisive shift in this direction occurred between 1896 and 1899. The present collection is comprised of excerpts drawn mostly from that period.[4]

---

2. For a discussion of this, see Christian T. Collins Winn, *"Jesus is Victor!" The Significance of the Blumhardts for the Theology of Karl Barth*, Princeton Theological Monograph Series 93 (Eugene, OR: Pickwick, 2009) 151–54.

3. Martin Stober offers the most complete analysis of this period of Blumhardt available to date. See his *Christoph Friedrich Blumhardt d.J. zwischen Pietismus und Sozialismus* (Giessen: Brunnen, 1998) 52–207, 259–71.

4. Jäckh's comments here need to be supplemented with the acknowledgment that some of Blumhardt's most significant "rethinking" actually occurred from 1890 to 1895 and finds expression in his *Gedanken aus dem Reich Gottes*, which was written at the end of these seminal five years. See Christoph Friedrich Blumhardt, *Damit Gott kommt: "Gedanken aus dem Reich Gottes,"* edited by W. J. Bittner (Giessen: Brunnen, 1992).

Blumhardt's new-found social orientation would lead him to the controversial decision to join the Social Democratic Party (SPD) in 1899, which he would eventually represent in the Württemberg *Landtag* or regional legislature from 1900 to 1906. As a representative, Blumhardt dealt mostly with issues of wage increases, trade tariffs, and education, though he also gave public lectures to church groups, explaining his understanding of the relationship between socialism and the kingdom of God.[5] Socialism was for Blumhardt both a sign of God's judgment on a culture that worshipped mammon instead of God,[6] as well as a sign of hope in which all people, but especially the poor, would share in the blessings of a transformed world under the reign of God.[7] Though explicitly atheistic, Blumhardt argued that the goals of socialism were a kind of sign of God's kingdom making itself present here on earth. In this sense, the socialists in their search for justice and relief for the poor were more Christian than many Christians. He thus envisioned his political work as a new form, but coextensive with what his father experienced, of the active struggle for the kingdom of God to emerge in history.

By 1903, however, Blumhardt's view of the SPD had considerably cooled due in large measure to internal party politics, and especially the personal attacks that Blumhardt was the target of during debates over Eduard Bernstein's revisionist program.[8] In 1905, due to failing health and

5. Most of Blumhardt's political speeches, as well as his speeches to Christian groups, have been preserved in vol. 2 of Christoph Friedrich Blumhardt, *Ansprachen, Predigten, Reden, Briefe: 1865–1917*, edited by J. Harder (Neukirchen-Vluyn: Neukirchener, 1978).

6. "Capitalism is the last enemy, mammonism. It kills . . . with *mammonism* everything now hits the mark. This is the anti-god, which can only be conquered by God" (Blumhardt, *Ansprachen*, 264).

7. "Whoever looks into the elements of social democracy and into the ideas which necessarily derive from it must recognize that a follower of Christ can very well empathize with it, actually more than with other political parties . . . A different order of society is sought for the sake of those who labor and are heavy-laden, for the sake of the outcasts and the downtrodden, for the sake of the infirm" (Christoph Blumhardt, *Eine Auswahl aus seinen Predigten, Andachten und Schriften*, edited by R. Lejune [Zürich: Rotapfel, 1936] 3:449).

8. For a discussion of the turbulent debates within the SPD over Bernstein's revisionism, see Carl Schorske, *German Social Democracy 1905–1917: The Development of the Great Schism* (Cambridge: Harvard University Press, 1955). Blumhardt came under fire for being sympathetic with Bernstein's revisionism. Though he had initially rejected Bernstein's program, after the personal attacks that Blumhardt experienced in November 1904, he came to see that his own position had more in common with Bernstein than he originally thought. See Klaus-Jürgen Meier, *Christoph Blumhardt: Christ, Sozialist,*

a more pessimistic view of party politics, Blumhardt decided to withdraw from public political life. Though Blumhardt placed less and less stress on political activity, he nonetheless remained committed to socialism until his death in 1919, believing that, at least in terms of its goals, it was indeed an anticipatory sign of God's coming kingdom.

In 1906, during a trip to Palestine, Blumhardt contracted malaria, which proved to be debilitating, further deepening his withdrawal from public life. Even out of the public eye, however, Blumhardt continued to exert influence through his publications and ministry at Bad Boll. His vision of the kingdom of God would prove to have a great appeal to a number of twentieth-century theological luminaries, most notably Karl Barth (1886–1968).[9] Blumhardt suffered a stroke in October 1917, which left him partially paralyzed, though he continued to attend services at Bad Boll. He passed away on August 2, 1919.

## BLUMHARDT'S THOUGHT

Blumhardt's thought is probably best described as a form of "kerygmatic theology." "Kerygma" is the New Testament word for "proclamation."[10] We use this descriptor for Blumhardt's thought first to refer to the lyrical, aphoristic, and sermonic quality of his theological ruminations. His oeuvre is nothing more than a vast collection of sermons, table-talk, letters, poetry, hymns, pastoral counseling, biblical commentary, autobiographical and biographical reflection, and a few public speeches. In fact, the *Gedanken aus dem Reich Gottes* constitutes the only sustained theological work that Blumhardt ever produced, and it is hardly a theological treatise.[11] The descriptor "kerygmatic theology" also evokes the practical, earthy everydayness that

*Theologe*, Basler und Berner Studien zur historischen und systematischen Theologie 40 (Bern: Lang, 1979) 107–10.

9. For a discussion of this influence, see Collins Winn, *"Jesus is Victor!"*; see also Markus Mattmüller, "Der Einfluss Christoph Blumhardts auf schweizerische Theologen des 20 Jahrhunderts," *Zeitschrift für Evangelische Ethik* 12 (1968) 233–46.

10. See Colin Brown, "Proclamation, Preach, Kerygma," in Colin Brown, ed., *The New International Dictionary of New Testament Theology* (Grand Rapids: Zondervan, 1986) 3:44–68.

11. For an analysis of this text, see Collins Winn, *"Jesus is Victor!,"* 129–36; and Simeon Zahl, *Pneumatology and Theology of the Cross in the Preaching of Christoph Blumhardt: The Holy Spirit between Wittenberg and Azusa Street* (Edinburgh: T. & T. Clark, 2010) 61–84.

marks most of Blumhardt's reflection and writing. His theology was forged in the heat of battle, whether pastoral, political, or personal, and this gives it a fresh quality and electric verve that still comes through today, a spiritual intensity that continues to feed those in need of nourishment. This quality also gives his thought a provisional and irreducible quality. The provisional character of his work refers to the constant need for theological supplementation, extension, elaboration, and clarification that confronts the reader of his works, while the irreducible character of his thought refers to the strange contexts and experiences in which Blumhardt's theological imagination was forged. Both Blumhardts understood themselves as witnesses of the in-breaking kingdom of God, and their witness and subsequent theological reflection retains an original, irreducible character.

But "kerygmatic theology" also refers to the non-systematic nature of Blumhardt's thought. One will find in his work theological themes and theses that stand in dialectical tension with no attempt to find resolution. The term "kerygmatic," then, is meant to evoke the sense of a loosely connected set of theological convictions that when assembled present a relatively coherent theology, a kind of theological constellation meant to provide orientation and guidance—though by no means a full-scale theological *mappamundi* (world map), since it retains persistent gaps, *aporia*, and even downright contradictions within the overarching unity.

That constellation of thought is established by two distinct poles, each of which is summed up in a kerygmatic slogan: "Jesus is victor!" and "Thy kingdom come!" Following in the wake of his father's thought, though with his own particular twist, Jesus' victory represents the pole of *divine action* in Blumhardt's thought. In other words, "Jesus is victor!" refers to the active presence of the living Christ, which is continuously invading the world of sin to free humanity and creation from its bondage to death, both spiritually and materially.[12] Blumhardt identifies this active presence with the kingdom of God. Jesus is the *auto basilea*: Jesus and the kingdom are functionally synonymous. Significantly, Blumhardt does not imagine Jesus or the kingdom as symbolic ciphers into which one can put any kind of content. Nor is it an ideal. Rather, the "kingdom" is to be understood according to the lines of the narrated life of Jesus as found in the biblical witness.[13] As such, in the moments of "in-breaking" there is both an element

---

12. Blumhardt's emphasis on the overthrow of death is especially prevalent in the *Gedanken aus dem Reich Gottes*. See *Damit Gott kommt*, 200–212.

13. See Collins Winn, *"Jesus is Victor!,"* 117–28; see also Gerhard Sauter, *Die Theologie*

of judgment and an element of reconciliation, which correspond roughly to the cross and the resurrection. That is why Christoph can be both prophetic and conciliatory in his preaching and analysis of contemporary events.

A key shift occurs in the younger Blumhardt's understanding of "Jesus is victor!" vis-à-vis his father. For his father, the living Christ not only forgave sins but also brought healing to the physical or psychical body. The son agreed with this, but extended it to the social realm. Contained within this extension was Christoph's conviction that social systems are also under the thrall of death and in need of liberation. The liberating work of Jesus, exemplified above all in his resurrection from the dead, is one that is to be universally extended to the nations, including the mundane social life of the peoples of the earth. This emphasis is especially pronounced during Christoph's direct engagement with the SPD and the Workers' Movement (1899–1906), though one can already detect components of this shift as early as 1895 in the later sections of the *Gedanken aus dem Reich Gottes*.

Sin and death are spiritual as well as social and systemic realities, but so also is the resurrection power of Jesus and the Spirit of God. For Blumhardt, God seeks a people who will struggle for the healing, resurrection power of the kingdom to be let loose in the cosmos. This people, who are both a product of God's calling and a result of genuine human response, constitutes the second key pole in Blumhardt's theology, exemplified in the watchword "Thy kingdom come!" God breaks into the world, but it is also incumbent on humanity to pray for God to act.[14]

Both the elder and the younger Blumhardt offered extensive commentary on the nature and practice of prayer.[15] Prayer is a complex and comprehensive act. At its most basic level, however, prayer is the straightforward act of "calling out" to God to act. The Christian life as a whole is itself an act of prayer, and in that act those who pray—or rather groan—hold creation up before the living God to ask God to renew and restore the earth.[16] Prayer, however, consists not simply of words, but of action.

---

*des Reiches Gottes beim älteren und jüngeren Blumhardt,* Studien zur Dogmengeschichte und systematischen Theologie 14 (Zürich: Zwingli, 1962) 24–45.

14. "All the great things which are to come, we shall already experience today quite certainly in all their glory if we pray and do not falter. But without prayer they will not come" (Christoph Blumhardt, "Our Human Right," in R. Lejeune, ed., *Christoph Blumhardt and His Message* [Rifton, NY: Plough, 1963] 218).

15. See, for example, Johann Christoph Blumhardt, *Das Vaterunser* (Basel: Basler Missionsbuchhandlung, 1946).

16. See Christoph Blumhardt, *Action in Waiting* (Farmington, PA: Plough, 1998) 99.

Christoph described prayer as "active waiting" toward the kingdom of God.[17] Ultimately only God's power can truly make a difference. Thus, we wait for God. But our waiting is also a hastening, for we are called to live out our faith in an anticipatory way: "Waiting means *action*—invading the shadows, surrounded by the most awful death, amid the angriest and most fearful clamor; for that is where the Day of the Son of Man is to break in!"[18] Thus, as we pray for the kingdom of God to come we anticipate the justice, peace, and reconciliation of the kingdom through concrete deeds of struggle, especially on behalf of the poor and oppressed. In keeping with his faith that only God's action will finally be decisive, our struggles for righteousness must always point beyond themselves. Though they may address the ills and misery we confront in the here and now, they achieve only relative success. Prayerful action therefore calls us to long and hope for the final coming when God alone will make right all wrongs. Our endeavors for justice, peace, and reconciliation in contemporary society can only function as sign-posts, pointing us toward God's final future. Nevertheless, for Blumhardt these deeds of hope help to draw the coming of the kingdom into history. Christoph also placed great weight on the fact that our calling to pray and to hope for the kingdom of God is a call to hope for God's mercy for all of humanity and the whole of creation. One prays on behalf of all people and all of creation, just as one works for social justice for all (even those who do not know or want to know Christ).

As described above, Blumhardt's "kerygmatic theology" offers a remarkably holistic understanding of the Christian gospel. Rooted in prayer, biblical reflection, practical living, and action, his witness contains an invitation to think, hope, pray, and act in the light of the coming kingdom of God. These are the defining marks of the church here on earth. Even if we don't always find ourselves in agreement with Blumhardt—needing perhaps to revise or reformulate this or that conception—nevertheless, for those with ears to hear what he seeks to express, the witness of Blumhardt will inspire and set in motion those who long for the coming of the kingdom of God.

---

For a more extensive discussion of this aspect of the Blumhardts, see Christian T. Collins Winn, "Groaning for the Kingdom of God: Spirituality, Social Justice and the Witness of the Blumhardts," *Journal of Spiritual Formation and Soul Care* 6/1 (2013) 56–75.

17. See, for example, Christoph Blumhardt, *Eine Auswahl*, 4:9–16.

18. Ibid., 4:14. Admittedly, Blumhardt would often go back and forth regarding the nature of "waiting," sometimes emphasizing stillness, and at other times emphasizing radical action. See Zahl, *Pneumatology and Theology of the Cross*, 74–76, 133–36.

## *Vom Reich Gottes*: History and Reception

*Vom Reich Gottes*[19] (*On the Kingdom of God*) was the brainchild of Eberhard Arnold, founder of the Bruderhof, and the editorial handiwork of Eugen Jäckh, Blumhardt's pastoral assistant and executor of Blumhardt's literary estate. In 1920, as Arnold was preparing to leave the Furche Publishing House to work with Otto Herpel and the Neuwerk-Verlag, he was already envisioning a series of volumes, including one on Blumhardt.[20] In the summer of 1921, Jäckh visited Arnold and the budding Bruderhof community in Sannerz, northeast of Frankfurt. Confessing that he felt a "spirit of kinship" with Arnold, Jäckh, along with Anna von Sprewitz, immediately set to work on the volume.[21] Over the course of the fall of 1921, the project ballooned into two short works, *On the Kingdom of God* (*Vom Reich Gottes*) and *On Following Jesus Christ* (*Von der Nachfolge Jesu Christi*[22]). Because *Vom Reich Gottes* was intended as an initial introduction of Blumhardt to the wider German public, Jäckh's introduction was included, and has been retained in the present edition as well.[23] *Vom Reich Gottes* was published in the spring of 1922 by the Neuwerk-Verlag, and was followed a year later by *Von der Nachfolge Jesu Christi*, which was published by the Furche-Verlag.

Both volumes were very successful, enjoying multiple printings during the 1920s and 1930s. Through these volumes, figures like Dietrich Bonhoeffer were introduced to Blumhardt's vision of the kingdom of God and his conception of discipleship.[24] In April 1940 Christoph Blumhardt's

19. Schlüchtern: Neuwerk, 1922.

20. See Markus Baum, *Against the Wind: Eberhard Arnold and the Bruderhof* (Farmington PA: Plough, 1998) 127–28, 147–48.

21. Eugen Jäckh to Eberhard Arnold, August 18, 1921 (unpublished letter; Bruderhof Historical Archive, Walden, NY, USA).

22. Berlin: Furche, 1923.

23. It should be noted here that Jäckh was aware—and critical—of Leonhard Ragaz's Blumhardt volume, *Der Kampf um das Reich Gottes in Blumhardt Vater und Sohn—und weiter* (Erlenbach-Zürich: Rotapfel, 1922). It is probable that he was made aware of the book because of Ragaz's extensive engagement with Blumhardt in the January 1921 edition of *Neue Wege*, the literary organ of the Swiss Religious Socialists edited by Ragaz. For Jäckh's awareness of Ragaz's book, see Eugen Jäckh to Eberhard Arnold, December 23, 1921 (unpublished letter; original in the Bruderhof Historical Archive, Walden, NY, USA). For a brief description of Ragaz's engagement with Blumhardt in the January 1921 edition of *Neue Wege*, see Mattmüller, "Der Einfluß Christoph Blumhardts auf schweizerische Theologen des 20. Jahrhunderts," 240–41.

24. See Jürgen Moltmann, *Sun of Righteousness, Arise! God's Future for Humanity and the Earth* (Minneapolis: Fortress, 2010) 233n1. *Von der Nachfolge Jesu Christi* is one of

works were outlawed by the Nazi Propaganda Ministry.[25] Here again, *Vom Reich Gottes* played a role, albeit a small one. In 1939 a new edition of the book was released, presumably under the urging of Jäckh.[26] On March 22, 1941, Jäckh received a letter from the Furche Publishing House in Berlin, along with a copy of the 1939 edition of *Vom Reich Gottes*. The letter indicates that the copy sent to Jäckh, "had to be presented to the Ministry of Propaganda" and bore the pencil marks of the ministry reviewer.[27] Next to passages like "As Christians we must expect God's kingdom—the reign of God on earth. Yes, even more than that, we must actively concern ourselves with it" and "Christ came so that God's lordship is acknowledged here on earth, so that his will is done on earth as it is in heaven" are clearly discernible pencil marks, indicating those points of Blumhardt's message deemed incompatible with Nazi ideology.

## THE PRESENT TEXT

The present volume is a recombination of the contents of both *Vom Reich Gottes* and *Von der Nachfolge Jesu Christi* in the attempt to capture the original vision that animated Arnold and Jäckh.[28] Some slight rearrangement has occurred, as the editors have inserted the three chapters from *Nachfolge* in between the third and fourth chapters of the original version of *Vom Reich Gottes* and have included Jäckh's original introduction as an appendix. With this new arrangement, it also seemed worthwhile to rename the volume, *The Gospel of God's Reign: Living for the Kingdom of God*, in an attempt to highlight that Blumhardt's message is far more practical than theoretical.

the books in the Bonhoeffer Nachlass (Nr. 299, Signatur: 5 C 10) housed at the Staatsbibliothek zu Berlin. Thanks to Ralf Breslau for this reference.

25. The order to cease publications was issued on April 26, 1940 (Original in the *Landeskirchliche-Archiv*, Stuttgart, Germany [LKA Stuttgart, D51]).

26. Eberhard Arnold had passed away on November 22, 1935. See Baum, *Against the Wind*, 252.

27. Furche-Verlag to Eugen Jäckh, March 22, 1941 (unpublished letter; original in the *Landeskirchliche-Archiv*, Stuttgart, Germany [LKA Stuttgart, D34, Bd. 88.2, Nr. 224]). Thanks to Dieter Ising for making a scanned copy of this available.

28. Even after Jäckh proposed a two-volume structure for the project, Arnold had serious reservations, because he felt that, without having all of the material together, the fullness of Blumhardt's vision would remain unexpressed. Eberhard Arnold to Eugen Jäckh, December 30, 1921 (unpublished letter; original in the Bruderhof Historical Archive, Walden, NY, USA).

The translation is the work of the Bruderhof community, especially Miriam Mathis. The Bruderhof, more than any other group, has been the central conduit through which the witness of both Blumhardts has been brought into the English-speaking world. It is therefore fitting that *The Gospel of God's Reign* should be the second volume in the *Blumhardt Series*, given its deep connection to the founder of the Bruderhof community and movement, Eberhard Arnold. It is to Eberhard Arnold that this volume is dedicated.

# 1

## God's Love

WHO CAN PREACH THE gospel with any semblance of hope if they do not know what God's love is in Christ Jesus? We are submerged in utter darkness. Our little bit of Christian culture is hardly enough to keep our heads above water. We are stuck deep in a morass of satanic and human affairs that hate the Lord Jesus. Jesus can "save" us when we die, but we think that on earth he should leave us in peace. Down here we have our customs and laws that can't be altered. However, the salient question is: "Can people dedicate themselves to God while they are still on earth?" If not, then the whole universe was created in vain. That's just why Jesus came, and that's just why we must do our part by saying, "Who shall separate us from the love of God?" (Rom 8:35).

What then is God's love? God's love is that he sent his Son to godless men and women with a definite promise, "Christ is the light of the world."

He brings peace on earth. It is through him that God's will shall be accomplished both for the individual and for the whole world. God's love is as broad and as great as humankind itself; it is as high and as deep as our misery, and more powerful than death—even unto the depths of the earth.

⊷

The world is a reality and can be overcome only by a reality.

⊷

To have faith means to feel God's presence.

⁘

The real meaning of faith is not a matter of reciting a Confession. Faith means to believe that something will happen, to believe that Jesus wants something of us, to believe that God's love can do something.

⁘

Knowledge of God must be experienced. You can never "study" God. If you know something of God and his love, you are greatly pained when people only philosophize about him. You think, "If you only knew whom you are talking about, whom you are dissecting, you would turn white with horror!" God has to be experienced. And whoever experiences him becomes speechless.

⁘

Don't place yourself above God with your intellect. Rather, put yourself beneath him with your heart. I pity people who find it so hard to have faith. Don't expect too much from them. We force on them too much that has become only history. Nowadays people seem to consider only with their heads whether they can believe. Their hearts are empty.

We have to come away from this intellectual religion that makes faith hard for people. Whatever makes your heart bow down before God's holy love is more important than anything you can grasp with your intellect. Forget about anything that does not touch your heart! But hold on to anything that sanctifies you, so that your heart becomes still before God. Not even the evil one can take that away from you.

Our hearts must open up to God once more. That's why we pray for an outpouring of the Holy Spirit. People no longer have a feeling for God. We cannot expect anything from them that goes against the way they were brought up, anything that goes against their culture or customs. But this feeling for God, this sense of God's love, is the first blessing we should seek to find for ourselves. There are many other blessings, but we must not want the last blessing first. If we can just take hold of this one bless-ing—the knowledge of God himself—then we shall proceed from blessing to blessing.

⟜⟝

There is a kind of disbelief that comes from reverence. The Apostle Thomas had too much respect for God simply to "believe." He knew that something as great as the resurrection could not just be believed as a matter of course. Many people cannot conceive that God would answer prayers—*but perhaps they are more devout than those who take it for granted that God answers prayers.*

⟜⟝

We human beings are always in love with ourselves and with our own thoughts and ways. We draw God down into our affairs, but always on our own terms. We think that God should act on our ideas, that Christ should come the way we want to go. This is why there are such terrible tensions be-tween Christian denominations and sects. Our human thoughts are stub-born—they make us rigid. For decades and centuries people keep going on in the same way, until finally they become hardened and cannot think otherwise. People become frozen in the ice of their own thoughts and ways.

God speaks out against this again and again and wants to tear us out of this condition. This is why the Savior speaks so sharply. He asks for judgment to help us glorify God's name. He calls forth events that throw our thoughts and wishes overboard. And so, according to God's will, time repeatedly sweeps over all our sterile thoughts. Nations and churches must collapse so that room is made for the thoughts of God.

⟜⟝

God's love is the key to the world we live in, the answer for those who seek for the truth. The world does not see God, but God sees the world, and whoever belongs to God also sees life in the world. And that life is the light of men.

⟜⟝

We dare not start with ourselves and say, "Jesus is my Savior—therefore he has also come to save the world." It is the other way around: "God so loved the world—therefore he also loves me. Jesus came to the world—therefore he also comes to me."

✺

No matter how high heaven is above earth, God showers his grace upon those who fear him. Though heaven is very high—and just because it is so high—it is near to us. The highest can become the nearest. We need something above us, which—precisely because it is above us—can illuminate things down to the smallest details. God's grace and goodness have to be very high so that we cannot tamper with them and so they can penetrate everything with light.

Many people would like God to be closer to them. They seek arduously for a relationship with God such as they may have with people. But even among people it is not good to come too close to each other—there are so many misunderstandings. Our spiritual worth and good qualities cannot develop freely if we come too near to each other socially. It would be all the more awkward, if God wanted to mix among us. He has to remain above for the sake of his love. As long as sin is among us, he must stay high above us.

Even Jesus has to be high above us in order to be near us. For, while on earth he was always eminent. He is high and exalted, but as such he is our neighbor. Being high above, he can approach all people and they can become one under him.

✺

From every pulpit and on every mission field it should be proclaimed: "You all belong to God! Whether you are godless or devout, under judgment or under grace, blessed or damned, you belong to God, and God is good and wants what is best for you. Whether you are dead or alive, righteous or unrighteous, in heaven or in hell, you belong to God, and as soon as you are swept into the current of faith, the good within you will emerge." Preach like this and you will have different results from those who preach the truncated gospel that gives with one hand and takes away with the other.

If only Christian wrath could be driven from our hearts once and for all! If only the passion for judgment and damnation would stop! If only we would learn to see sin as a disease and to separate the sinner from the sin! Our faith must be a light from God that draws people into the stream of faith. Then the most godless will become righteous.

God loved us even when we were his enemies. If God loved you when you were still a sinner and drew you into the stream that led you to himself, then how can you damn others? Surely it is only a matter of time before they will also enter the current of faith. But if we throw obstacles into the stream, if we have "Christian" or religious misgivings, how can there ever be a current that sweeps up other people?

⊷

All of us belong to God. That is the gospel. Once this good news is understood, sin falls away. The gospel must no longer be combined with threats. We cannot lay any obligations on people—unless they have already come to God. If we want to be true evangelists of the gospel to those who are bound, then the gospel must be, as with Paul, a power from God, not a speech or a command. The gospel is a power, not merely a message. Therefore we must keep it pure. To combine the gospel with threats makes it unclean; light and darkness get mixed. The apostles' message was pure; it was those who came later who added threats to it.

God's original message was, "You belong to God." God defends the rights of humanity. God is love. In other words, he cannot accept the thought of even one single person not belonging to him. Right now people live in darkness, but they will all be freed. That is why we, too, must also defend this right for every person. To condemn anyone upholds the power of sin and death. As soon as you condemn someone, you deny God a certain right. You must commit each person to God's care and keep him in mind as one for whom God's right will also come to light, or you are not a disciple of Jesus. And you must believe the same for yourself. That is the gospel.

⊷

Our righteousness consists in this, that we belong to God our Father, and that we look upon ourselves as belonging to God the Father. This is the essence of true human nature. Even to a person in hell you must repeat: "You belong to the heavenly Father!" He who no longer counts himself as God's is unrighteous, but as soon as he realizes that he belongs to God, he regains his true nature. This knowledge strikes through all sin and death, even hell itself. A person who knows, "I belong to God," will overcome everything because God overcomes everything in him.

You belong to God because Jesus lives—not because you are a Jew or a Christian, but because Jesus lives. No devil has rights to anyone, only God! Certainly you may have to suffer now; but in your hell, in your misery, even in your death, believe this, "I belong to God." Then God will make you his son, his daughter, and put you in his pocket like a lost coin or take you in his arms like a lost sheep.

The prince of this world has succeeded in concealing this gospel, and thus this great news still remains hidden. But one day it will go through the earth like a storm.

⊖

God wants to be kind to us, and his goodness is always available to us. But we tend to be pessimistic, like certain leaders who often direct the currents of contemporary thought toward pessimism. But most people actually want to be joyful, and since God comforts them, they find happiness again and again.

As Christians we ought to rejoice when people are happy, not get annoyed as soon as they are cheerful and deny them every pleasure. Rather we should lovingly encourage such joy. God wants to do people good, and so we, too, should rejoice when things go well for them. God wants to bless us. He did not create us for torment but for struggle. And in this struggle we should feel joy again and again, for God repeatedly tells us, "You are, after all, my child!"

Without the awareness of God's goodness, we remain stuck and go under. Despite sermons about damnation and hell, we must realize, "God loves us." Wherever this realization penetrates, people do not rest. The ultimate religious question breaks through national barriers, for wherever Jesus is present, true progress thrives among the people. People revive when God's goodness is recognized and felt. "The gospel will be preached to the poor," so even the poor are comforted.

The goodness of God in Christ can be seen in Jehovah's relationship with the people of Israel. The Gentiles stood under God, too, but the people of Israel lived under Jehovah—the one, who dwelt with them. Originally this name meant nothing other than the cry: "He is here!" When Jacob rested on a stone and saw the ladder to heaven, it meant: "He is truly here!"—and God's goodness showed itself in special love and deeds of kindness.

In Christ, however, God has come fully into the flesh. Through him you may hope in this great goodness of God, a kindness that penetrates the deepest human misery. Yes, it reaches right into hell, for Christ also "descended into hell." There is no place, no situation, to which God's love does not have the right of entry. Therefore no one should ever consider himself lost, for there is no lock that Jesus cannot open.

"The Word became flesh"—and when we grasp this, especially in our sinfulness, it justifies us and cuts us off from the sin in the flesh. Then there will be a new flesh: one flesh with Jesus Christ the Savior. That is why Jesus calls himself the resurrection and the life. If formerly your flesh housed the working of sin and death, now there dwells in you the one who makes you alive. Jesus lives and God's goodness takes up residence in your flesh and kills sin.

"The Word became flesh." If that news lives in you, you will begin to have a heart that sings. Pain will come, but you will sing. Sorrows will come, but you will sing. Death will come, but you will sing. Never let this singing be taken out of your heart. Keep singing, and then you will shine forth light. Sing, however dark it is. Praise God, thank him, and glorify him. Jesus lives—and we live too.

Fear belongs to the laws of the state, not to the gospel of Christ.

We fallen humans lie in the dirt—yet we are precious stones. A diamond that lies in the dirt cannot glitter. But because it is a jewel, it cannot be spoiled by the dirt. It can be picked up and polished again, and it will still be a diamond and sparkle as before.

Therefore, when you find yourself lying in the dirt, don't think that you are a rotten person. *It is a crime against God's love to think of yourself or anyone else as being bad.* What God has created is not bad. But we can find ourselves in the wrong place, and because of this, what we are gives a completely wrong impression. If the jewel is to sparkle, it must be brought into the light somewhere. If we are to "sparkle," we must be in touch with

7

the light. That is why you should not just tell the unbeliever that he is a sinner. First you have to tell him, "God loves you!" Sin begins when we no longer remain faithful to God. It is a sin if the jewel, having once been cleaned, throws itself back into the dirt. If a person knows nothing of God, however, we should not speak of sin, but of misfortune.

⟜

A lie gains real power once you believe in it, when you willingly throw yourself into it. Sin would be nothing if it did not immerse the whole person in deception—as if it could separate us from God.

Even in the time of the apostles, the Antichrist stuck out his tongue at the gospel with the false statement: "Whoever does not abide by the Law is a sinner." For example, in his First Letter John campaigned against the Antichrist and proclaimed: "Believe in the Son; for whoever believes in the Son knows that he himself is also a child. So now, be a child in regard to your own sins and shatter this lie—as if your sins could separate you from your Father! You cannot fight against sin until you are free of fear through the Son."

⟜

Sin confuses our awareness of what is true; it makes us think we are living somewhere different from where we actually are. We are in God and have eternal life, yet when we sin we live as though God and eternal life did not exist. The root of sin is our failure to live in harmony with God's love, which always surrounds us. But when God gives us grace, the veil is lifted, and we recognize God and experience eternal life.

⟜

To stop despising ourselves and other people—that is the foundation for all moral and social life. There is no lasting morality without this foundation. Only on this foundation can there be peace among ourselves and among nations. The nations must learn to respect and value each other. Likewise, no genuine social life can be supported without this mutual respect. Therefore, we have the good news of God's love—that God loves this poor, godless, unredeemed world. This alone is the precondition for every true culture and morality.

⤸

My father once wrote to me that I should make it a rule, wherever I go, to regard nobody as an unbeliever. Because of his love, God has faith in people, and thus we should also have faith in them. This is really possible. People come to faith because God has faith in them; you and I have access to Jesus because Jesus has come to us.

⤸

Our faith corresponds to God's love. God comes to meet us, and then our hearts well up with love to God. God approaches us as a loving Father, and thus he is no longer some great, high, unapproachable, and inscrutable Being. He is a fatherly protector wherever we go. From within us, our faith responds to the Father—and faith is no more than holding tight to the love that we, as children, have received from the Father.

Faith is what mounts up from the earth. Love is what falls like rain from heaven. God wrestles for this faith on earth. Our goal should be that among us this faith wells up like a spring. Never doubt God's love! It never ceases. Just as God can never cease to be, so his love can never fail. No one can loosen himself from God's love—even if he were the worst of sinners, he would still be connected to God. On God's part, his fatherly love will always be warm. That is why Christ came into the world: so that we would know that love never ceases. Why do we preach Christ if at the same time we condemn ourselves and throw ourselves or others away? Why then did Christ come into the world? Every person can and should come before God and say, "Father, from your hands I came forth, and only good comes from your hands, and so my prayer for your Spirit shall be heard and shall come true."

Whatever tries to come between us and God must perish. God's love from above, our faith from below—and whatever is in between must be crushed. From this marriage of our faith with God's love emerges a true person. We must still go through struggles. It is good when we have to fight hard, because then evil is placed between our faith and God's love, and that is the place where it must be dissolved. It is precisely when evil gets stuck between me and God, that I find out who I am, that I find God's goodness in myself, and that I find righteousness.

⤺

Abraham became righteous through his faith. By throwing everything that we humans purpose to the winds, he took his stand on the side of God and freed himself from the whole domain of sin. Righteousness does not consist in my not making any more mistakes—it consists in my whole being harmonizing with God. The sun is just, whether it has sunspots or not. The righteousness of God reposes in every created being.

If we grasp the concept of righteousness, we will realize that righteousness exists solely in relationship to God. Nowhere in creation does righteousness exist independent of God. Therefore we must not seek to be good in moral codes, but in our relationship to God. Moreover, we must not judge others according to their behavior but look beyond that to their relationship with God. Many a person, though not really aware of it, has a great deal of righteousness deep within him. His spirit simply does not yet take part in the latent righteousness within him.

Now Jesus comes into the world and regards people as righteous. He forgives sins because he regards us as righteous and believes in our relationship to God—even though we continually tear it apart by our foolish actions. Our wrongdoings produce what looks like a vast separation between God and us, and so millions of people believe that they don't belong to God. They think God has rejected them. So much of our unhappiness stems from this opinion. If we could only eliminate this way of thinking, then everyone would be enormously uplifted; people would become "righteous through faith."

⤺

When we read the parable of the treasure buried in the field, it makes us want to pray, "Dear Father in heaven, help us to find the hidden treasures of the kingdom of heaven." If we search and dig in the field of life, we will find the hidden treasure. Even in today's circumstances, where everything appears to be confused, where everything is bent on distressing and oppressing us, where everything looks bad—even here, suddenly we encounter the reign of God. Even in our afflictions, in our anxieties, needs, and struggles,

God is there! There is a treasure in them. Therefore sell everything you have and buy the treasure. Cast all your troubles and woes aside, and seek God in whatever situation you are in.

This is how the Savior lived on earth. He did not recoil from the world—not even the wicked world, not even his enemies. He found God the Father even in what was bad: "Thank God! The Almighty is in the world. Now I know why my Father sent me into the world—it contains a treasure!" Jesus goes to a wedding and finds treasure there. He goes into the wilderness, is surrounded by hungry people, and he finds treasure there. He experiences anxiety, need, and struggle and finds treasure. He is hung on a cross and groans with pain, he descends into the grave and into hell, and he finds treasure. Father, Father, Father in everything!

Can we do likewise? Yes, that is what we pray for: "Let us find you, God, in all things." Should we hang our heads—we who stand by the Savior? Must we lose heart? No, no! Whether we are hungry or satisfied, crying or laughing, we have treasure there, and because of that we can forget everything else. Where is our heavenly Father? He is in the world, in the distress, in the anxiety and our darkest need, in all our troubles. Have no fear, the treasure remains, for we belong to our loving Father in heaven.

✧

We stand between light and darkness. In light resides life, and in darkness, death; in life resides goodness, and in death, evil. This conflict brings us into terrible need. It is the principal mystery on earth. But God is above light and darkness, and we can turn to him in everything. He is the one and only, and as soon as anything besides him wants to take control, it thereby becomes evil. From God's viewpoint evil is evil, and darkness is dark, because they have lost their connection to him. Darkness exists only apart from God, not in him. Because God is perfectly good in himself and because everything good in creation comes from him, everything must be called darkness that does not allow itself to be placed in harmony with him. From his point of view it must be called dark and evil.

If we think about this it should bring us great consolation, for in the end, darkness, too, is completely dependent on him; evil, too, is not beyond God's control. Evil cannot exist in and of itself. We can reckon that the whole world, including sin and evil, is in God's loving hands. There are *not* two worlds—the one in God's hands, the other not. Even where it is totally dark, God alone is Lord. No devil can do just as he pleases. He dwells in the darkness at God's command. He has a certain life there that is unfortunately infectious and death-bringing for those who let themselves be drawn to it. But the whole realm of sin and death remains in God's hands.

In Christ, God loves the world, the godless world, the world that has fallen under Satan. "The people walking in darkness have seen a great light" (Isa 9:2). The despairing, the condemned, the slain, the wretched (for whom there was no more consolation), all these have been permitted to see the Father who loves them. God has seized control of the darkness, and it is a loving control. Now it is no longer as it was before: "A dreadful thing to fall into the hands of the living God" (Heb 10:31). For God has seized control over sin, death, and hell through his love.

If we, as disciples of Christ, let no other lord have dominion, if we refuse to believe in the devil, but instead give ourselves to God and his love, if we can exclaim, "Jesus is victor, and there is no lord of darkness who does not have to bow down before our Lord," then darkness will melt away. We must push the darkness out of our own hearts and out of the world, by not allowing anything but God to rule, and by standing firmly on the gospel of Jesus Christ. We are God's.

When we look at the world, it appears as if everything Jesus wants is impossible. We rebellious human beings are striving after completely different things from what God wants. We are enmeshed in disbelief and ignorance of God. Because we do not understand God, we fabricate some other ruler for ourselves. This, in turn, leads us to disobey God even further. Certain powers then come into being that express themselves in customs and habits. In following these, and in our disobedience, we become unhappier and unhappier. The Chinese man who buries his child alive or walls up his children in the Great Wall so that they will be safe, the Hindu woman who throws her child into the Ganges, the millionaire who is consumed with making more money—none of these people are happy. They are slaves, not masters. God has enclosed them all in the misfortune of unhappiness, but he does so that he may have compassion on them, so that the hour may come when they recognize that only he can help them. For God can withhold his help for only as long as we think our happiness lies elsewhere.

Nothing can be done with a self-willed person bent on crime except lock him up. But God never does that. When we disobey God, we create our own prisons. God has nothing to do with hell—it is *we* who prepare it for ourselves. God is ready, always ready, to break up any hell if we want him to; but we have to want it. If we remain stubbornly bent on living apart from him and do not acknowledge the divine that seeks to work within us, our obstinacy will lead us to create our own hells.

There are visible and invisible hells, but such prisons of torment are not places. A place in and of itself has never made anyone accursed. There are people who live in the most miserable places and are nonetheless blissfully happy. Yet we do create tormenting circumstances through our self-will and stupidity. And we will continue to do so if we are not enlightened by God, who alone can lead us to life.

Even to the Pharisees Jesus said, "The kingdom of God is in your midst." Why? Because in his love he refuses to let himself be severed from anyone, not even from his bitterest enemies. He sees them as in bondage, but he also sees in them the seed of God's kingdom. In Jesus, God has planted a seed within the human race. This seed must sprout in each individual so that the kingdom comes forth from each person—from you and from me, from Jews and Gentiles, from the devout and the godless. This will be the marvel when God's kingdom appears: it is not the work of anyone great, but it is something living that thrives and grows from millions of people.

# 2

# The Reign of God

As Christians we must expect God's kingdom—the reign of God on earth. Yes, even more than that, we must actively concern ourselves with it. We should not think about ourselves or our religious destiny. Christianity is not like other religions—its prime purpose is not to make *us* happy. Rather, Christ came so that God's lordship is acknowledged here on earth, so that his will is done on earth as it is in heaven—and then, naturally, we shall also be blessed. Until then there is no blessedness, except the blessedness that Jesus experienced on the cross and that fills our hearts when we suffer need and death for our Lord and king.

✦

Jesus is God's oath—his way of saying: "I promise you with this man that the world is not lost, that humankind as it was meant to be can come into being, that in your very flesh, of which you nearly despair, the light shall dawn."

Why did Jesus heal the sick, raise the dead, and perform miracles? Was this not more than a mere doctor's service or a momentary display of fireworks? If his works were done only at the beginning, to arouse the enthusiasm of his disciples, then his life is one great deception. If Jesus' life, with its signs and miracles, has no eternal meaning, no promise that help will be given to us while on earth today; if I am to receive help only when I die or only in heaven, and the earth is to remain cursed—then all the words of the apostles are worthless.

No believer can be used for God's kingdom unless he trusts in the power of Jesus to gain God's victory here on earth, to make sinners righteous, and—rather than damning the godless world—to redeem it from its godlessness and help it toward eternal life.

↬

Earth is not excluded from the biblical hope for the future. Earth is the locked paradise, the paradise that is closed to us. Earth is the heaven that belongs to us human beings.

Creation, as described in the first chapters of the Bible, was not finished. It was "very good"—that is, very good for its future development. The first humans were "perfect," but only as an embryo is perfect. In the beginning, humankind lacked the bones of its spiritual life, so to speak, and was still supple. Humankind was completely pure and holy, like a newborn child. Then their development began. Starting from Eden, man and woman were given the task to conquer the earth. Everything was very good, but now, "Arise! Create your paradise and fight for it." Had the first man and woman remained obedient, they could have started this work in their immediate vicinity, under God's protection and guidance, and worked out from there. There would still have been struggle, but it would have been far easier.

Of course, who knows what good fortune lies hidden in the fact that humankind has had to mingle with the unhappy and unfinished spiritual condition of the earth? Perhaps through this, our struggle will reach deeper and achieve a more thorough perfection. But certainly it will be revealed one day that God held everything securely in his hands.

In spite of sin, we are still called to conquer the earth. "Fill the earth, and subdue it." Our paradise is hidden in the earth. How happy we shall be, when we can sense "the goodness of the land" (as the Bible says), the spiritual goodness of air and water, earth and heaven! How joyful we shall feel! If I am obedient, I will be surrounded with blessings already now on earth. But if I live a life of disobedience, I will only be able to perceive half the fragrance of God's goodness. I will not be able to live fully. How often we are saddened by spring, when all around us new life is stirring and we are not a part of it. We also need to be rejuvenated each year—like heaven and earth—and lead lives in the strength God has bestowed on us. Instead we have to bear sickness and misery in the prime of life. Moreover, we take the good things out of the earth at great cost to our lives. How much blood clings to the coal we burn? If we wish for paradise we do not need more progress in chemistry and physics or more comfort for our daily existence. We need God's Spirit.

God created the earth through his Spirit. Spirit, therefore, penetrates everything, including the material world. But we have not yet discovered this Spirit. Nor do we have the Spirit of God in ourselves as we should, and so we do not perceive him in our material existence. All things thirst for the quickening breath of God. But this Spirit does not come if we ignore the simple commands of God.

Therefore, don't desire to do outstanding things. Live simply and justly. Wherever you find yourself at present, see how you can obey God. We must regain confidence that we are able to know his will and live according to his kingdom. If you make mistakes, you will learn by them. Trust and be faithful, and then God himself will come to meet you. Encourage everyone and say, "You also belong to God. Get up and give yourself to him." Together let us belong to him—then at last the good things of earth will follow us, and earth will become our paradise. What we will then have to do, as people of paradise, we do not know yet. The first thing, however, is to become people of paradise, to learn how to live wholly from the Spirit of God, as our inmost soul requires.

❧

God wants to be king on earth, as Isaiah promised: "The Almighty will reign on Mount Zion and in Jerusalem" (Isa 24:23). God wants to be the ruling principle everywhere and for us to do his will voluntarily and joyfully. God wants to reign in Zion, and Zion is on earth. He wants to be among us on earth, so that everyone may sense his presence and direct their life according to God's will.

The prophets saw all of this quite clearly. But when we think about it, and wonder what it will be like, we are mystified. We are used to thinking of God as being far off, up in the skies somewhere. That God should make a difference in our daily affairs is outside of our experience, and so we push this thought aside. Yet God is waiting for us to make a start, to make room for him to reign. He not only needs people who do not oppose him—he needs people who get things going. He needs volunteers who allow themselves to be led by him in everything. Even if we are sitting in a train, we can be in tune with his intentions. We can be shopkeepers or peasants in tune with his intentions, or husbands, wives, or children. Then we will be blessed.

As of yet, however, God does not freely rule among us. Other things have our attention, God is merely a postscript. Other things govern our lives and yet we expect God to give us his blessing. But it is God who must reign, and only then should other things be added. Our whole sentiment should be: "Honor God! Look only to God! Don't look to anything else for direction!" Because we nowadays chase after other things, we make stupid mistakes and our eyes remain closed. But we must in faith place God upon the throne, so to speak. Then his blessings will flow into all corners, even the smallest and most insignificant.

⊕

What matters is that people are delivered, cut free, and torn away from false masters, from human domination. God's sovereignty opposes human dominion. That is the point, and that is why the struggle in us and around us is so hard. If God's kingdom exists only to give us joy in heaven, if we were meant simply to put up with the way things are and accept all laws as they are, it would be an easy matter. Then all we would have to do is accommodate ourselves to the world. We could stupidly accept that our whole history of war and hatred is part of God's order, that violence quite naturally belongs to human life, and that without war there would be no real men. After all, "Christian" nations go to war in the name of God. We oppress each other in his name, and in so doing the world remains the world. There thus arises a world god, whom the Savior calls the prince of this world. He claims our allegiance. But Christ, too, claims our service; he rises up in the name of God and shapes life on earth in opposition to that power that has established itself over the centuries. This is why it is such a struggle for God's kingdom to advance on earth.

⊕

When God's kingdom comes, a strong wind will blow against all sin—that is, against the merely human order that exists in rebellion against God, anything exalted and human made.

⟡

We should never say, "That cannot be changed." Whoever says this is far from God's kingdom. People who are content to let things continue in the world as they are, who always bemoan, "You can't do anything about that!" prevent God's kingdom from coming. Such talk is the big enemy of the kingdom. It paralyzes the new life that wants to come on earth.

⟡

Do you believe in God's kingdom? Then get ready to be unsettled! God's kingdom is good, and you know you are not good. God's kingdom is truthful, and you are entangled in lies. God's kingdom is just, and you operate in a world of injustice. God's kingdom is full of love; it is merciful, even toward its enemies. What about you? Without even realizing it, you have become as hard as stone. Should you therefore give up? Many people despair of the goodness and mercy, the truthfulness and justice of God's kingdom because they themselves cannot properly take part in it. Indeed, God's kingdom should make us conscious of our sin and wretchedness. His kingdom should unsettle us, but we should not despair.

⟡

There is a certain level of enlightenment in the world today, which acts as a preparation for the kingdom of God. There are new recognitions in the sphere of human endeavors—some that have never been achieved before in our struggle for civilization. Never before have the laws of nature been so well understood as now. Never before have we known so much about the starry heavens. Never before has the earth been explored to the extent it is today. In the space of a few decades, our material lives have changed. This is partly the result of the Holy Spirit at work, who comes near to earth as progress is made.

As a result, certain weighty questions are now being raised: How can we really become human? How can we build mutual relationships that make life on earth truly tolerable? How can peace be achieved among the nations? These questions, among many others, often get ridiculed—especially by Christians. But it is easy to scoff. As Christians we should take part in these struggles. Think about it. After thousands of years such questions are now raised: How can we abolish war? How can we abolish poverty? What has inspired people today to ask such questions? This comes from God. These thoughts are good, and all good thoughts come from the Spirit. People around the world are voicing them, and if we Christians won't speak up, then unbelievers will.

⊸

The difference between the Holy Spirit and our human spirit is that, whereas all human spirits rely on force, God's Spirit does not. God's Spirit seeks to set us right inwardly, so that we ourselves find determination and accomplishment. God's reign touches our innermost "I," so that it freely unfolds toward life.

The Holy Spirit is at work everywhere. It is not a spirit of churches and confessions, parties and nations. The Spirit belongs to all humankind. It is the Spirit before whom all the differences between us, though they do not disappear, become meaningless. Yes, human society could be like a lovely forest in which firs, beeches, oaks, tall trees and undergrowth grow peacefully together, presenting a unified whole. It could be arranged with great variety, in differing stages of development, yet as one glorious living organism. But that is possible only through the Holy Spirit, which makes us truly human in our relationships to one another.

Therefore in the latter days of the Holy Spirit, what is universally humane must come to rule. All people must be educated inwardly toward peace and mutual respect and guided into battle against hatred and evil. They must be freed from the opinion that they are fundamentally evil. They must win courage for what is good—in themselves and in the world. And then what is genuinely human, which is also the divine, can find expression in worldly people. Without having heard anything about us, they may be able to bear in themselves the truth of God.

Naturally, when the Holy Spirit comes there is also judgment. Sharp judgment has already been passed on our age. Our time is one of revelation, a time in which the hearts of men and women are being laid bare. Good and bad are coming to light. The more the Holy Spirit comes to us, the sooner will the liar be stamped a liar, and no title or famous name can protect him.

The Day of the Holy Spirit is slowly being prepared, and although people still do not desire it, they will have to desire it; although they do not understand, they will have to understand. Although they are so foolish as to think that humankind will find ways to progress without God, they must become changed people. The Spirit of God penetrates all heights and depths; he sweeps every corner clean. As the Spirit of Jesus Christ, who is the Savior of the world, he will guide all people.

⟜⟞

After his suffering and death, Jesus presented himself to his apostles and gave many convincing proofs that he was alive (Acts 1:3). Jesus proved that he was alive, that he was Lord. God always shows himself to be a living God. Human progress toward God is rooted in this fact that God shows us that he lives. But the ways in which he shows himself are different at different times. We are not likely to experience it the way Abraham did. For Moses the way God revealed himself had a special character that accorded with the needs of his time. God disclosed himself in a different way to Samuel than he did to Isaiah. It is always different, yet always the same: God shows himself to be a living God.

This is the greatest grace there is on earth: the possibility of communication between us and God. If I wish to speak with someone on the telephone, he or she must also have a telephone. If God wishes to show himself as the living God among us, there must be someone somewhere on earth who is able to receive him. This is the greatest grace: that again and again at different stages, in the most terrible circumstances and darkest times, there have been people who had this receptivity. Again and again something pure and innocent shows up among people and directs us toward God. Earth is covered with a blanket of sin and death, but all at once a light breaks through somewhere, and communication with God is possible.

God is always at hand; he despises nothing. If a heart shows itself to be only a little bit receptive, God is able to do something, revealing himself as the living One who is present. He does not hesitate to approach unbelievers, too. At the time of Socrates, Plato, and Aristotle, God revealed himself, though naturally according to the context of that time. Despite the whole outlook of those days—when for example slavery was considered essential, as it was even in the time of the apostles—God revealed himself in such a living way that we, in our time, still draw on it. God was able to reveal his glory also in the brutality of the people of Israel, at the time of the conquest of the land, and later among the kings.

God continues to speak today. He frees us from old conceptions. Therefore, we must not cling to anything. Today we may think that this or that is absolutely impossible, but by tomorrow we may think very differently. Today we may fight lock, stock, and barrel against certain theories and systems, but then tomorrow we may feel compelled to accept them. Recall what a tremendous struggle there was against the abolition of slavery. Today, however, in America and Africa slavery is deemed inhuman. God will put an end to everything that does not belong in his kingdom. The way God revealed himself in former times always agrees with the way he shows himself today. Of course, how God reveals himself in our time is not exactly the same as in the Bible. Today God is speaking among the nations, and thoughts of what is good, just, and humane are stirring. God is using strong language—holy, true, and merciful for the whole world.

The light that shines through human beings is the only light that can reveal God's kingdom on earth. Abraham, a simple caravan leader, received the first revelation of God for the salvation of the nations. The Almighty does not come down from heaven as an extraordinary phenomenon—the Father himself comes to us quite simply in the form of a person who is his instrument. Sinful men and women always try to separate God from this light of revelation. They are obsessed with finding a revelation that is spectacular. Despising the revelation of God as it comes to them in human guise, they fall for deception and illusion, for spiritual phenomena that draw them into the realm of the supernatural. But this human trait of seeking divine revelation outside the realm of human experience has ruined all religions.

We have to understand how we have arrived at this self-contempt. We human beings are, so to speak, an unbaked loaf of bread; no person is finished. And now, unfortunately, before we are complete, we have become conscious of our existence, and our incompleteness embarrasses us. We are like a caterpillar that strives to become a chrysalis. We feel bad for ourselves and can hardly bear our imperfection. And because we do not listen to the voice of God, who loves us imperfect beings just because our imperfection is on the way to perfection, we arrive at self-contempt and give ourselves up as lost.

The world's religions are preoccupied with the "world above" and do not understand the material form in which God appears. Thus Jesus, in his holy material existence, is "destined to cause the falling and rising of many, and to be a sign that will be spoken against" (Luke 2:34).

Certainly one thing today is encouraging: there is a thirst for what is genuinely human. People are striving to become more humane. The world no longer tolerates heartless people who try to pass as pious. To love all people, to love the world, to despise and condemn nothing—this is what is paving the way for God's kingdom in our time. This is from Christ and precisely why he became like one of us. Since he took on our flesh, no one, and no class of people, can be despised anymore. We must hold onto this revelation of God, seeing in every person the image and likeness of God. After all, "Goodwill toward all people" was proclaimed at Christ's birth.

People often suppose that God spoke only in Bible times and that he no longer speaks today. He does speak today, but in Bible times the people were more childlike and sensitive and understood how to distinguish between what came from God and what did not. People were more on the watch and listened more attentively, and therefore they could hear God better. God's language is finest when it wells up through our own childlike spirit, when the divine streams out from within us, as out of a rock. Such utterances of God uplift, sanctify, and transform our very person.

God's blessings do not simply fall from heaven like dew. There must be people who allow themselves to receive his blessing. God's powers are always there, but they cannot always be focused. He reigns, but if we want the bounty in field and forest to be harvested, there has to be a farmer or two. God cannot bless your cattle, but he can bless you—and with you, your cattle, too. Without someone who has surrendered himself as a vessel to God, no blessing can come. But when someone renounces himself for God, for truth and right, his prayer can be blessed by God.

In our praying we make many mistakes. It is typical and naïve to pray: "Bless my field! Bless my cattle!" That is heathen. Some people, who don't care a hoot about God, nevertheless expect God to bless them with all good things. That's what the pagans do. Eventually they castigate their gods if they do not do their will. But God needs people on earth who want and do what he wants—stewards, servants, and maids—and if he has these he can give his blessings and hear their prayers.

⊷

God reveals his glory differently in different times and in different people. With Moses there was something terrifying in it, for his age was coarse and brutal—the peoples had to be hauled through the coals, as it were, and the glory of God appeared as a consuming fire. But in Jesus we see the glory of God as the splendor of the only begotten Son, full of grace and truth, full of inner warmth and kindness. The consuming fire of the old is extinguished. Now the glory that overcomes evil with good is revealed; not the glory that shows itself in anger and wrath, in the fervor of Elijah, but rather the majesty that sets everything right in the soul.

This glory awakens faith in those who are humble. Faith is but the reflection of God's glory, just as the light of the moon is a reflection of the sun's light. Because the sun shines, so does the moon; and because God's glory manifests itself, so does our faith. If the glory of God shines forth, so can faith shine forth in thousands and millions of people.

Today it is of the utmost importance that the light rises in our hearts, as the Bible puts it, that "the morning star rises in your hearts" (2 Pet 1:19). Even the light of Venus, the morning star, is but a reflection of the sun. From within, radiating outward, the world must be enlightened, and out of the innermost core of life the power of renewal shall come forth. Nothing is really achieved through external wonders and signs. If they do happen, people just look up for a moment and then carry on as they were before. Until the brightness of God's glory rises in our hearts, even the greatest miracles will be of no value. But once the light of God arises in our hearts, miracles and signs will appear as a natural consequence.

⊷

Miracles are not abnormal phenomena; rather they create normality. There are many forces within nature we know nothing about. God's potentialities are limitless through the laws that govern creation, and so he is able to remove evil, even quite suddenly. Ask any doctor and they will tell you that they experience things with their patients that they don't understand. One patient dies, another gets well, and they don't know the reason for either. We see and grasp only the most obvious of God's natural laws.

If we are waiting for the world to be freed from the destructive disorders and abnormalities of life, then the innermost laws of life must be uncovered—not merely the laws of physics and chemistry, but the laws that lie at the heart of nature, at the place where we perceive the driving force that is so miraculously at work in the whole of creation, including ourselves. Every person senses what lives in him and what does not live in him. If the secret energy of his life ebbs, he cannot do anything. If he does have this energy, he still does not know where it comes from. We are inwardly dependent on certain laws that we do not comprehend—God came in Jesus in order to reveal them to us. Jesus is God's Son because he knows who God is and what he does, and he stands at the center of the laws of God's kingdom.

If there is to be progress in the world, the Almighty must intervene and his inmost works must be revealed—otherwise we will remain in our misery. Everyone who communes with God lives from these powers and reckons with them. It is from these powers that the "mighty works" of which Jesus speaks are made possible (John 14:12). But are we capable of receiving these great powers? Were we truly a church of Jesus Christ, we would surely no longer need much of what doctors still find necessary. There is still so much in the world of which we know nothing.

⊕

God has always worked miracles before which we must stand in silent awe. When God pursues his cause, everything baffles us, at least as long as the channels of our human understanding are blocked. We can even get annoyed at the things God is supposed to have done. We are ashamed to admit that miracles are even possible. But there have been miracles since the beginning, and they are always the sheer wonders of *life*.

We live but on the decay of former ages. The Alps, for example, reveal many strata of past worlds, all of which no longer exist. They were imperfect—there was something desolate about them. It is wholly upon the ravages of water and the wastelands of fire (upon all that has been burnt up, washed out, and petrified) that our lovely world has come to be. Wherever God appears, he appears in renewed life. Whenever the sun shines after a rain, whenever spring follows winter, the creative deeds of God show forth, and humankind is refreshed. This phenomenon can be so powerful that a sensitive person almost hears the rustling of the first creation. Each one of us is called to live amidst God's creation with this understanding. We must enter the place where God said, "Let there be light!" Only then can our souls rejoice.

Within this divine stream, made up of miracles of life, a dead and dying world is placed—our human world, which is like a corpse laid in a fresh spring where the fish play and water flows over it. Whoever dwells within the corpse notices nothing of the pleasant, clear water. But this dead body must be revived, restored to inward and outward health. For this to happen new miracles are necessary, but these are the very miracles people object to most. They do not deny the wonders of creation, but they do reject these new miracles, the miracles based on the restorative powers of God. God wants the corpse to come alive again. The Savior enters into our dead, human world, and through him resurrection is proclaimed. We who have become part of the corpse and are ourselves decaying hear the word, "Let there be light!"—and behold, we live. Our eyes and hearts are opened, and we see once more the fresh waters of creation.

Think then of the Savior who is at work in this dead world, and you will begin to grasp the meaning of his life's battle. Think of his church in the midst of stinking humanity. We almost go under, yet we do not perish because Jesus is victorious. And how does he conquer death? With the doctrine of justification through faith? With any other doctrine of salvation? No, with resurrection! Jesus lives within this corpse and gives entrance into the corpse for the cleansing waters of God.

As Jonah cried out to God from the belly of the whale, so must we cry out from the belly of our fallen humanity, "Jesus lives! Resurrection must come. The Almighty lives. Jesus is alive. He is Lord!" In the midst of death we are embraced by life that wants to flow in. Where everything is numb and dead, miracles of life take place, and then new stories unfold from which the history of God's kingdom is made. A little of this is written down in the Bible, but it is not a millionth part of what people have gone through who, in the midst of death, were taught by God so that they could proclaim the miracles of life. It was impossible to write down all that Jesus experienced or all that God was in Jesus. For the present, the Bible must suffice. The main thing is that we are alive, that we are resurrected right in the middle of the corpse. Then not only shall we be able to testify about divine miracles, but we shall also experience them ever anew.

⊸

We are wonderfully made by God. Therefore, it is not good always to look for God outside of yourself. Seek him, for once, within yourself—you are a whole world of miracles.

The most wonderful thing is that human beings have to struggle for everything. We have to prepare our food, cultivate our fields, and work for everything. It is a marvelous thing that we have to be creators ourselves. Animals remain what they are, but we are able to take the path of growth. And in Jesus, our brother, the incarnate Word of God, we can see this growth and its progress before our eyes.

We must again and again begin with the simple recognition that we are children who are destined to become something. We must experience a new beginning, a rebirth, a *different* birth. The wonder consists in this, that today I can be such and such and tomorrow I can start quite anew. This is not so with an old tree, but it is so with you.

Jesus Christ is the new power of creation. In him God's kingdom breaks in. In him you can begin again, and on the basis of this fresh start, you can experience remarkable growth, just as Christ, who despite anxiety and tribulation, need and death, did not regress but moved only forward to the resurrection. And surely even beyond the resurrection there is always new growth until the unfolding of the greatest glory of humankind. So now we may look at what is broken and see perfection, at the sinner and see righteousness, at someone in sorrow and see his joy. We deny God's existence the moment we think that we, or anyone else, have to remain as we are now. Nothing remains as it is: God is the living Lord, and under his rule wickedness ceases, and imperfection is transformed into perfection. As little as God can die, so little can you be kept pressed down. We are creatures who in God never stand still. You are like a grain of wheat that may lie in a granary without germinating for a long time, but then all at once it falls into the right soil, where God touches it and it grows.

Therefore, act now! If you are unhappy, rejoice until you are happy. Things will change—you have a right to it: things will change. If you are facing death, then rejoice in your life, and it will be different at the end. If you are stuck in the mire of sin and filth, don't bury yourself—things will change. Our humanity stands above nature. Stones, plants, animals—everything lives and moves, but we as God's children grow into eternity.

Every world has its own consciousness, including the earth. The consciousness of the earth is humankind. But until humankind has recognized the Son of God it is still night on earth. For Jesus is the light of the world. To be sure, he is already a certain light in those who are his, but this light is only like a small lantern. It will remain night as long as Jesus is not recognized by the whole of humankind.

Today we are still only prodigal sons, children who have not yet come to true consciousness. But we are God's children. "You are all sons of God," says Paul; that is, we are all made in his likeness. When Jesus enters the flesh in the name of God, he comes into something kindred to himself. He cannot enter something unrelated. Existing in human flesh, he is aware that he is God's very own—the Son of God. Every human being needs to come to this awareness. In this consciousness we can defy the whole world, for with it we are stronger than the whole world. And once we have this true awareness of self, we can arrive at an abiding awareness of God. Then we will be saved. Those who are saved are a light in the world. When we are filled with God's Spirit, there will be light in the world.

This consciousness of who we are as human beings is being born in our time. It is making itself heard; it is surging up from the mire of millennia. The night is advanced, and the day draws near—the day on which Jesus the Lord will appear and transform all consciousness of self into consciousness of God.

Our faith in Christ includes a measure of faith in humankind—the belief that through God, through the Spirit of Christ, through the Holy Spirit, humankind will arrive at something worthwhile. Our faith must achieve something, namely what human society has always striven for, but cannot seem to obtain. We have to believe that humankind will be able to represent something of God's eternal kingdom upon earth. We shall not perish in distress and misery. No longer will it be a disgrace to be human—it will be an honor to have become true men and women again, free from all dishonor.

A yearning for this lives within every human breast—a primeval yearning that cannot be destroyed. Jesus came in order to satisfy this longing. As surely as Christ was born, and as surely as his gospel is preached, one day God's kingdom will come upon earth. As Christians we must believe in the future of humankind.

⌖

We will only become happy when we make others happy. This is actually our true nature, just as it is God's nature, so to speak, to be happy, in that he loves humankind. Is it really fanatical to believe in the thousand-year reign of God, to believe that this divine impulse within us will be victorious one day?

⌖

We are "born"; other created things are "made." Originally we came from the earth, a "lump of clay," as the Bible says—related to the animals, as science maintains. But God's spirit was breathed into us, and so began the struggle for the spirit within the flesh. The "animal" in us still seems to have the upper hand, and it costs us a tremendous effort to hold firmly to the spirit born in us. But the divine in us wants to be satisfied. We must assert the child of God that is in us against the animal in us. For through us God wants to penetrate the whole sphere of creation with his Spirit. Only in this context does our life's battle have meaning.

It would be senseless to concern ourselves with human misery if it were merely a matter of saving a few people. No, we have a calling: as children born of the Spirit we must permeate the whole of creation with the Spirit.

Human beings belong to the *God* who created heaven and earth, not to the created heaven and earth. We have completely forgotten that all people are born of God. Even though we have forgotten this, we are born of God still—this birth remains even in the most depraved people. This is what demonstrates God's love in Jesus Christ: that he holds firmly to this birth of humankind. That is why Jesus must be God's Son. And anyone who takes away from Jesus his right of Sonship and his right to reign robs from himself the privilege of being born of God.

# 3

# The Living Christ

JESUS IS THE SON of Man, the true human among humanity.

⊸

What is the "glory of the Son of God"? The glory of the earth is what makes it the earth, the glory of the sun is what makes it the sun, the glory of an oak is what makes it an oak. Likewise the glory of the incarnate Son of God is what makes him a man. In Christ the glory of humanity appeared for the first time.

⊸

John says in his Epistle: "Whoever does not confess that Jesus Christ has come in the flesh is not of God" (1 John 4:3). With this he is saying: Jesus dwells now in humankind; he desires to be among us. You must appeal to this "Jesus in us all," to Jesus in the flesh as the one who is righteous and who preserves righteousness for the whole world. If you do not do this you are not on the right path and you will not have strength to live for the kingdom of God.

⊸

Let us sing praises for the great kindness of God in sending the Lord Jesus into the flesh. If Jesus had not entered into our impurity and our sin, if in his holiness he had removed himself from us—where would we be? Let us sing praises, too, for the millennia of the past. Time and again, God has entered world history with all its sins. God has allowed the brutalities of the ages, all the pride and desolation of humankind, to be loaded onto his shoulders. God made use of David, even though he had fallen deep into impurity. He used Nebuchadnezzar, too, as well as the stiff-necked Israelites. He even worked through the Greeks and the Romans. God has gone where every kind of sin has been committed.

Some people find God's involvement with human sin quite troubling. So much so, that today there are those who even find fault with him, as though God were a sinner! If he were really just, they claim, he would never have blessed people who are full of sin. Why has he taken on himself the disgrace of our folly? Doesn't this make God responsible for the crimes of war, for all godlessness and deceit in human history? But God the Father has remained among us just because he loves humankind and wants to lead us out of our sinfulness. It is through his very presence in our sin that we shall find the strength to grow into the light of truth.

Jesus came into the flesh as the Son of this Father. He has entered the most depraved areas of human life and provided spiritual guidance in even the most gruesome of "Christian" eras. Think back to the days of the barbarian invasions, when wild tribes gave their allegiance to Christianity and marched through the land shedding blood. Consider the crusades, when people thought it the noblest of deeds to slaughter the Turks. What savage years followed the Reformation, during the Thirty Years War, when Jesus was supposed to have accompanied Gustavus Adolfus to war. Jesus at war! Jesus killing people! O dear friends, what has he *not* taken upon himself over the course of the centuries? Consider how many situations caused by *your* folly he has entered just to hold onto you. If the Lord Jesus had let you go your own way, you would not be here today.

Jesus came into the flesh and continues to enter into it right up to the present day. He takes upon himself all kinds of shame and deceit. In all the false directions taken by the Christian church, he has held on to God's tiny thread and fought quietly for the honor of God, so that even out of misguided human movements some of God's truth might still be revealed. That we are able to praise his name today, and that he, as the one Lord in heaven and on earth and beneath the earth, is able to hold high the banner of the kingdom of God, is due to the fact that Christ continues to live in the flesh.

Yet, let us always remember that Christ remains the Holy One. When Jesus lived with his disciples he went everywhere with them, also to tax collectors and sinners. Then he died and was gone. But afterward he rose again, promising that he would not forsake humankind. However, the risen one is now different than he was before. When the disciples saw him after his resurrection, he was different; there was a distance between him and them. He was and is holy.

Jesus judges the world by withdrawing from us. We must learn to accept this judgment, too—and be content to remain firmly in fellowship with Christ but through the Spirit only. When the time is right, Jesus withdraws and the sinful person inwardly collapses. The time is coming when Jesus will again leave us. But then you must follow him. For this is what the last Day will entail—not Jesus coming into the flesh, but humankind entering into his Spirit. It will not be like it was before. Jesus will no longer take up the cross, when he bore every humiliation. In the last days Jesus will blaze the trail, and you will have to deny yourself and follow him. Then it will be revealed who belongs to him and who does not. The faithful will enter and the doors will close behind them.

This is how Jesus will judge the world, but this is also how he will heal the world. When he departs from us as the risen one, our flesh collapses. But that, in turn, leads to our healing. We are stuck in something that must first break down. There is such a foggy atmosphere that surrounds humankind that even when Jesus enters it the light still does not shine through. Therefore a time must come when he stands beyond this fog, this spiritual cloud that causes us to sin again and again and that torments us.

So let us rejoice when Jesus opens the way to the Father. He will surely give us the strength to follow him. In the last days it will be outwardly a difficult time, but inwardly things will become easier. This will be the time of Christ's resurrection, when his light clearly shows the way into the kingdom of heaven. With or without suffering, this trail to the Father will be blazed. And this Father is the very one who restores us as his people. He liberates us from ourselves and changes us completely into purified beings.

⊷

Christ came in the flesh in order to combat sin in the flesh. "Christ in the flesh" means that God's righteousness opposes our "righteousness." It leads to the fight of life against death. Christ did not come to bring peace upon the earth, but a sword. Christ's peace is a matter of taking part in the battle, like a soldier who has no peace as long as he lies down and sleeps in his tent, but only when he joins in the conflict.

"Christ in the flesh" gives us hope of becoming truly human. Because Christ is in the flesh, we no longer have to be slaves of sin. The sin that dwells in me can be driven out, and then God can dwell in me. Once this happens, I am a true human being, and I am then able to love all human beings, the whole of creation, for all flesh belongs to God.

Since Jesus took on our flesh, all people will recognize him in the end. God will rise up like the sun among the races. It will happen differently among different people, but Christ will make all races into one people of God. Life will not be dictated according to our Western culture but by the needs of each race. God will enable us to love even our enemies—whoever they happen to be.

Jesus does not do battle with our flesh, but wages battles in our flesh against all darkness and sin. He fights in us, not against us. And this struggle will continue until all of humankind comes to know him, who is God's victor over sin.

In the confusion of our lives a new way has been shown us through Jesus Christ. This new way does not hinge on our birth or upbringing. It depends on a gift from God—his appearance in his Son, who as the highest and divine human being can intercede for all human beings. We should not take away from the Savior the fact that he is the Son of God. And didn't God create us human beings in his image? If you say it is impossible for Jesus to be the Son of God, then God is not your God—he is a god, but not *your* God. But if God is our God, then he can give to us in his Son something divine that sets us on a new way.

People have made Jesus the founder of a religion. No! He is the bringer of life.

✧

Most people have given up hope of ever becoming new. Regardless of how many despair of this possibility, we believe it and must tell others about it. In Christ we are a new creation (2 Cor 5:17). Christ wants to create true men and women here on earth. Jesus came to fashion people full of the power of eternal life, people who have God's love within them—the light of truth and the light of life. If right from the start we Christians had been true to the Lord, our world would be very different. Let us therefore put on the new "man," which is being renewed in knowledge in the image of his Creator (Col 3:10).

✧

Jesus is our advocate.

✧

Most people do not really live. They are tired. They trudge through life on a wrong basis and are thus not genuine about who they are. They are in-sincere—both in their happiness and in their sadness, in their poverty and in their piety. How refreshing it is to meet someone who is simply himself, even if he seems somewhat rough and unrefined in his ways.

Jesus lives. He says, "I live! In me you can see an example of life." This word alone has an enlivening effect. Just looking at someone who is truly alive gives one strength for life. Just to see a doctor who is full of confidence can help a sick person. Jesus tells us: "I live. Look at me. Look until you are satisfied. For you, too, must live—that is why I am in the world."

Life itself has something infectious about it. Just as disease-bearing germs spread, so do miracles of life, especially those wrought by the Spirit. This is why Jesus can turn the world upside down. He is light in his very person, and contact with him is contagious. Expose yourself to this conta-gion. Become alive! Jesus does not require arduous intellectual effort—no, a creative power emanates from him that renews us. He wants to be more than a unique example. In other words, he doesn't want us to be mere hangers-on, clinging to him like leeches. We must become alive ourselves.

Jesus always remained himself, whether he was with tax collectors or with Pharisees. He had true life within him. Therefore, society did not infect him, rather he infected society. And we, too, should be alive like that: people with life, who are sent into the world. When we are alive we can determine whether something is genuine or not. A person who is alive sees the truth; he somehow knows whether or not to get involved with this or that situation. He has sharp eyes and ears and possesses a fine sensitivity for things that are not worthwhile, taking no part in them. He can distinguish between God and mere material influences.

If we wish to make an impact on the world, we must be alive. Unless we are inwardly awakened, our theology is useless. It is our life alone that makes any lasting impact. When we are alive, people take notice and say, "Yes, there's something living in him!" Only then do we have a right to go to people and be a witness.

Of course, all this requires a certain renunciation. We must let go of the things that appear to have life but in reality do not—customs, traditions, institutions that are held in respect but are dead. I do not mean renunciation in the monastic sense. Jesus does not turn his back on the world, as if the blessings of this earth were evil. He simply wants us to find the life that is in him and then spread it to others.

⌖

Jesus is the servant of God. As God's servant he "will not shout or cry out, or raise his voice in the streets" (Isa 42:2). That is, he does not join in the boisterous, competitive spirit of our age. You will not find him where people hate and condemn each other, where they struggle for higher status, or where people seek to be more important than others. He is someone who gives up his life for the sake of others. This servant is tenderhearted and humble. He walks gently in our midst, seeing in every person something of God that must be saved.

This servant is "a covenant for the people and a light for the Gentiles." He shall "free captives from prison, and release from their dungeon those who sit in the darkness" (Isa 42:6–7). This is why people still wait for him today. This is also why his voice must sound forth again on earth. The time must come when the gospel is proclaimed in the fullness of its true meaning. But for this to happen the gospel must already be living in those who represent Christ on earth. A person with God's kingdom at heart—with all nations at heart and not just his own nation, with all generations at heart and not just his own family, with all people at heart and not just himself—such a person is bound to have a true understanding of Jesus Christ.

⟿

Jesus comes into our world as the Lamb. When he was on earth he lived in absolute subordination to the rulership of God, even unto death. This is the nature of the Lamb: the complete renunciation of every human achievement. Salvation comes only by surrendering everything that is human in complete submission to God. There is rejoicing in heaven over the Lamb who found the way to set everything right. In Revelation this Lamb breaks the seals, and with the eyes of hope, we already see every living thing being brought back to God. Every heavenly being exclaims in anticipation, "Praise God! Right will prevail! Blessed be God and the Lamb!"

But who understands this Lamb? Christianity? But our Christianity fights for its own existence just as much as Islam or any other religion—and, consequently, the Lamb stands isolated in heaven. We have lost the radicalism of Jesus, who put everything into the Father's hands and who chose to die rather than stir one finger to do evil. The Lamb's standpoint has become foreign to us. The seals of God's judgment are not broken by heroes, though Christianity has produced plenty of heroes. No, Jesus needs people who place their whole lives, as he did, completely into God's hands.

⟿

On Good Friday people typically stream into churches. Hundreds and thousands, who normally never go to church, attend church on Good Friday. These same people may actually scoff at religion, but on Good Friday they come. This is significant. Without their knowing it, the crucified Savior is their hope. Therefore, we must not criticize such "Good Friday Christians." Instead, let us thank God for the fact that the Savior is still drawing people to himself, because in him the Father loves the whole world, this world that is so "lost." And yet this very world cannot help but sigh in longing. So, let him who sighs turn his gaze to Jesus Christ.

꘏

Jesus went the way of suffering and did so in the same strength in which he lived, in the same power in which he gave sight to the blind, made the lame walk, and preached the gospel to the poor. Both his life and his death are the result of divine power. This is why he has such a tremendous effect in the world. Indeed Christ's death is the driving force of a different world history. We gladly preserve the memory of this or that person's life, but we prefer to forget their death. With the Savior, however, it is the reverse. His earliest disciples remembered his death, and ever since, it has become a great blessing for the world. Even today we know of nothing greater than the crucified Jesus. Perhaps we find it difficult to grasp or explain how the blood of Christ should make us blessed. Nevertheless we sense something of its power, and we look with longing eyes upon the suffering and death of the Savior to see whether it may become a source of life for us.

Even if only a few grasp the significance of Jesus' death, the power of God in Christ still affects the whole world. For through his sacrifice, sins are forgiven. His death has the power to overcome death itself, that is, to form us into new men and women. This power puts an end to our erring, mortal, and transient natures. All that is earthly in us disappears, like smoke, when confronted by the cross. And through the cross God becomes mightier and mightier until he is all in all, at first in his children, and then in the world. Light streams forth from Jesus' death—a radiance that will one day illuminate the whole world and lead everyone into a completely new life.

꘏

"In Christ we have redemption through his blood, the forgiveness of sins, in accordance with the riches of God's grace" (Eph 1:7).

God be praised and thanked! We have deliverance. What happiness there is for a prisoner about to be killed to realize: "Help is coming! I've been heard! I am freed!" Such vibrant joy as this grips us whenever we look upon the Savior. In him we have redemption, salvation is on the way. We are powerless. We lie down and languish and cannot escape from our distress. But he is strong—the victor who can wrench us out of our need. He alone has the power to free us from our misery.

But we must remember that we have redemption at the cost of his blood. Why through his blood? Isn't God's power sufficient to deliver us from evil? Couldn't the Savior's blood have been spared? Those who think this way do not realize how much the following words apply to us: "You will certainly die" (Gen 2:17). They do not realize how bound we all are in Satan's dreadful embrace, and how we can escape it only when our sins are wiped out and our blood is freed from its bondage to sin and death.

That is why the Father in heaven said to the Savior: "Go down to poor humankind. Your pure blood has the power of life to wipe sin away from the impure blood of human beings, so that they, the impure, may live again with you, the pure." And so Jesus sacrificed his life, and his blood was poured out to reconcile us to God. Because his blood is pure, it remains living even in death. Every drop of our blood is bound up with sin, and so we are weak and powerless to overcome sin. But the Savior's blood stayed pure; he has the power to lay down his life, and he has the power to take it up again. He possesses the Father's promise: that his blood can free us from the bonds of evil and death.

Now, because the blood of Jesus has touched ours, our blood can, so to speak, sigh with relief and be filled with hope. We can cry out: "O Jesus, have mercy on me! Help my sinful nature to have life! Grant me life, reconciled, cleansed, and set free from death. I give myself to you completely."

With the death of Christ a new road is opened to us, a new covenant begins in which we can be freed from our preoccupation with ourselves. Upon the soil of the old covenant, human efforts produced much that was fine and noble, but in the end the world gained nothing. Thus when Jesus came to gather his people, they were not ready. They were not free of themselves, and remained in their human pride and self-love, in all their human activities. Along this old road there is no real forgiveness, no true justice. The human element, which makes a person try to control his own life, grows too strong. The whole foundation of his life must be changed.

Christ's death throws all our good human efforts "to the winds." Even within "Christianity," human accomplishments achieve nothing of lasting value—not even with the utmost piety or the most orthodox faith. We still think that if we try very hard, give up worldly pleasures, and obey all sorts of commands, we will find peace with God. But this is still the same old road—whether I in my own strength have "faith" or in my own strength "perform good works," it is still the old way. The new road, the new covenant is not understood.

This is the meaning of the new covenant: "I will step aside and let God act." Christ surrendered everything into his Father's hands, and draws us with him onto that same foundation. That is where our sins can be forgiven, for only there can they be destroyed at the root. For the root of sin lies in our stubborn resolve to live independently of God. Human nature itself is not evil, but when we separate ourselves from God we start to rot and from this rottenness all sorts of hateful things seethe to the top. Only when we are in touch with God can we be made right again. And this takes place through the blood of Jesus Christ alone. Who shall rule? Christ's blood cries out: "God! The will of God!" When God rules in us, sin ceases, and so does our stubborn self-will.

⊸

The significance of Jesus' suffering and death comes to light only when the outer events of his suffering are over. A person's life story does not consist solely in what we see from the outside. What is great and important is the light that shines from him even after his life is over. This is especially so with Jesus. What has come to pass since Jesus' earthly life belongs to the history of eternity. It should penetrate into our time so that our earthly history is overshadowed by the truth. Behind the curtain of world history stands the cross and resurrection of Christ. Now and then the curtain parts and the crucified one reaches into our world through judgment. Who is able to continue in his sins, when the curtain parts and the crucified Christ manifests himself? Who can maintain his vanity, in this transitory life—in his own flesh—when confronted by the story of the cross? The cross silences us.

We must pray for God's judgment to come again and again. It is not a judgment that damns or destroys, but one in which even the worst evildoer can hear, "Father, forgive them for they know not what they do." We must plead for the power of the cross to manifest itself in our time. "Father, let the judgment of the cross of Jesus be revealed. Let our arrogance and pride be shattered so that the horrors of the past will never recur. And may the bestial and murderous spirit of humankind be overcome through the miraculous power of the cross." It is from this cross that the mighty cry resounds, "Stop, proud world! Your end has come!"

It will be a great victory when Christ no longer has to come to us in judgment. When the raging nations no longer do as they please, when our selfish pursuits are countered and our hearts are made more sensitive to God, when we are horrified at our own cruelty and ashamed of our baseness—that will be a great and glorious victory! We hope that the cross of Christ will win this victory in our time.

Jesus' death was not a heroic sacrifice as the world understands it. A hero surrenders his life in determined self-will for the sake of some idea or lifestyle. But the driving force behind Jesus' death was not obstinacy—it was the genuine power of life. That is the amazing thing about the cross. The path Jesus followed was not human but divine. Only God can transform suffering and death into a holy power—a power that can change our daily lives.

To be sure, Christ's crucifixion is still an offense to many, as it was for Peter. There are those who think that to accept suffering and death means to give up all activity and stop striving for something better in the world. But Jesus told Peter not only of his suffering but of his resurrection: "On the third day I shall rise again" (see Luke 9:22). His very suffering and death actually have power—the power to stir new life. Christ established a new law. Whatever normally cripples our strength is transformed into something alive and life-giving. Our inner being grows strong through suffering and death.

The purpose of Christ's death is to bring the law of resurrection into our poor, weak lives. The mystery of the cross is that it transforms the destructive power of death into a revitalizing power of life. Mere dying is no mystery, but death *as life* is a mystery. And this mystery must be revealed to this poor, dying world. Then there will be no more reason to lament suffering and death. We will instead be able to see triumph in them.

The shroud of death will not be removed as long as we merely sympathize with the agonies of Christ, or simply react with indignation to the many evils that we encounter. We can't rebel against dying; the law of death and the law of life coexist everywhere. Creation is always in the process of dying. But here lies a hidden mystery; death comes from the same God who gives and affirms life. When a tree's leaves die, the tree can again draw strength into itself. When we die outwardly, we can indeed gain strength for life—for eternal life. That is the great task set before us through the death of Jesus.

Christ's cross is a mystery. No new life can be given to us except through this great work of God, the work that leads from death to resurrection. Only the cross of Christ will overcome the world. Let us welcome this cross into our hearts, then come what may—die what must, perish what is destined to perish—we will suffer and die and still be victorious, because Jesus Christ is living with us.

❧

Jesus was patient even unto the cross. And he persevered because he was rooted in God's love for the world. But think about it. It is terribly hard to be patient unto death. Every disciple knows what it is like to grow bitter when adversity comes his or her way. Again and again we lose the patience of Christ. That is the reason we experience so little of the resurrection. Christ's patience led him to the point where his accusers thought, "He is done for"—and just at that moment the powers of resurrection shone forth. And only in the resurrection can the kingdom of God envelop the earth.

❧

The Savior can help the world precisely because he died and rose again. To our human eyes it is impossible for someone who no longer visibly exists to achieve anything. But Jesus takes God's cause completely out of our hands to show that *God* alone is the one who can accomplish it. Only his work—the work of the heavenly Father—endures. Therefore Christ's death is no hindrance: he rises again. He leaves the fellowship of humankind because he wants to prevent us from coming too close to him. He chooses a sphere where no one can tamper with his person. Only as the risen one does he become the Savior of the world.

❧

Jesus has no successors as other men do. He is the risen one. After Moses came Joshua, after David came Solomon, but in this sense Jesus has no successor to follow him. After all, he lives on! He is the risen one, the one who lives forever. And just because of this we can say as Paul does: "I no longer live, but Christ lives in me" (Gal 2:20). Because Christ lives, he can dwell in every person, including you. Through him the actual power of God enters into our lives. This power can come into every person, for "here there is no Gentile or Jew, but Christ is all, and is in all" (Col 3:11).

We must fight for this. Only one Christ. One Lord, one faith, one baptism! As soon as any person is given equal significance along with Christ, Christianity becomes a historical phenomenon which owes its development to others, rather than to Christ—then we are lost. Then darkness falls and unbelief sets in.

We do not have a religion, we have the living Christ. Christ lives—that is the great difference between him and all others. And if we have Christ himself as the living one, we need no laws or statutes.

But where Christ lives and reigns, something new happens. Things no longer follow their ordinary course. Where Christ is living, we must await his command. And he *can* give a different direction today than he did yesterday. He can cure a sick person with a word, but he also has the freedom to say, "Today it is better that you endure your sickness." He is bound by no rules. But something wonderful always happens in his presence, wherever a human heart enthrones him. Our hope lies in this living Christ.

Because Christ lives, everything must come right. No one should say: "I have wasted my life. My life is a failure." God, in Christ, can set right the worst of bungling and mistakes. Because Christ lives, we humans can again and again fight our way through to victory. Once the whole world conspired against Jesus—they said, "He shall not be born, and if he is born, then he shall die, and if he nevertheless lives, then all kinds of difficulties shall beset him!" And yet he was born and he rose from the dead and still lives. There is the same opposition today against the church of Jesus Christ: as soon as people become like Christ and live like him, everything conspires to oppose them. But yet they live, because God is with them.

Believe in God! Believe in Christ! Only then will the kingdom of God break in. For only Christ can bring about the reign of God in the face of all circumstances. Nobody and no church can achieve it. Only Christ personally can bring in the kingdom of God in which neither good nor evil can take place apart from the rulership of God.

Therefore: Let not your hearts be fearful. Christ lives!

⤏

When my father took up the watchword, "Jesus is victor!" it was a radi-cal stance. He was surrounded by a Christianity that merely repeated the words, "Jesus has died." He himself was very much involved in this kind of Christianity. But suddenly there burst from him: "Jesus lives! Jesus is victor!" And the devils fled. All the mystical and pious gloom around him was dispelled.

A true hero is with us, Christ, who drives everything else from the field and gains the victory, and through him people are saved. A person held in prison needs someone to come and break the bolt and lead him out. Once the prisoner has been freed, his sins are forgiven. He now has a brother who teaches him, who introduces him to different ways so that he can be cleansed of the dirt still clinging to him from the habits of his old, dark nature. The grace of Jesus Christ becomes a transforming power for us. The healing grace of God has appeared and disciplines us. Every day we get a "box on the ear" to help make us change our ways. We receive a new education in the school of Christ so that certain things, which are current in the world, gradually become impossible for us. Through our relationship with the living Christ we acquire different habits, customs, and ideas.

⤏

This is the name of Jesus: the guarantee that good will be victorious.

⤏

It is impossible for us, as humans, to bring about what Jesus accomplished. True, our struggles and efforts to follow him are not in vain—they will cer-tainly bear fruit. But he must be there to give the last blow, to complete the whole. That is why he is known as "the first and the last." We lie in birth pains between this "first" and "last."

The "last" Jesus, however, is different from the "first" Jesus. He is no different in character—he is just as humble and meek as the "first" Jesus. He is just as full of God's love to the poor and needy. But he is greater and mightier than the "first." He is now the risen one who since the time he was on earth has been at work in heaven gathering power and glory. And when he is revealed as the "last," he will appear as the Lord, King of kings, who rules over all things decisively. We await with joy the one who, as the "last," will be great in the hearts of us men and women.

It is our good fortune that we cannot find total contentment. None of the inventions of the last centuries have ever made us happy. We seem to always be hankering after something different. We actually do not know what we are longing for. We simply cannot be content. We will be satisfied only when we truly enter into what our Lord is, what Jesus is (the Lord of creation)—we will be happy only when we enter into this light of life in which we, as children of the heavenly Father, see ourselves united with all living things. As long as we are separated from earth and heaven, separated from a real life in God, we will be unhappy.

It is hard to convince people that what they are lacking is the risen Jesus. They often think of happiness in terms of money or honor or success, and thus remain depressed and do not master their fate. They let themselves be controlled by daily events, instead of finding mastery over their circumstances through Christ. Therefore, a person is fortunate whenever they realize that a real change must come. In this way they meet the Jesus who says: "Behold, I am making everything new" (Rev 21:5).

It is our good fortune that we cannot find total contentment. None of the inventions of the last centuries have ever made us happy. We seem to always be hankering after something different. We actually do not know what we are longing for. We simply cannot be content. We will be satisfied only when we truly enter into what our Lord is, what Jesus is (the Lord of creation)—we will be happy only when we enter into this light of life in which we, as children of the heavenly Father, see ourselves united with all living things.

We are living in a so-called progressive age. We see all kinds of developments—one invention and break-through after another. But in spite of this, there is no real improvement. This intoxication with progress is actually slowly passing over, and thus we feel ourselves parched. In the end we are still very human and have nothing unless we have God as the highest good. What are we without the good, righteous, true, and eternal? What benefit is all the clatter of machinery and all the exhilaration of activity? Neither technology nor science can help us toward what is eternal. For this to happen, the church of Jesus Christ must arise, and in the end Jesus himself must come again.

We desperately need the Lord Jesus to appear *in person*. Even in everyday human affairs, nothing truly gets accomplished unless there are individuals who spend themselves with their whole being. Similarly, we cannot keep propagating Christianity simply "in the spirit." Somehow or other Jesus himself must touch and move us. Just as the personal presence of a great commander brings victory, so the Lord Jesus must make himself felt in flesh and blood.

This can happen, for the Savior has received the power from God to say "*Ephphatha!*" ("Be opened!" Mark 7:34) to every form of human bondage. This command, "*Ephphatha!*" has to precede him and prepare the way in our hearts. What must Peter have heard to make him say, "You have the words of eternal life." "*Ephphatha!*" had pierced him. He was able to see and hear God himself in Jesus. That's why he could say what he did. People, even Gentiles, came to Jesus and begged him: "Lay your hands upon this poor person." In a childlike way they thought, "If Jesus touches him, he will be healed." What must they have heard beforehand to give them such faith? "*Ephphatha!*" This trumpet call preceded Jesus through the land.

In some way or another, all those who say, "Jesus, help us," must have already heard "*Ephphatha!*" because in their cry for help they lay everything else aside. Most people waver between two kinds of help—the help of God or human help, spiritual help or the help of spirits. This is what gives rise to superstition, which doesn't quite trust God and therefore turns to other means. Humanly, we do not manage a simple, straightforward "Lord, lay your hand on me." We need grace to accept God and Jesus as our sole redeemer, discarding everything else, so that our senses are not continually clouded over, making us unable to grasp who God and Jesus are. The revelation of God must precede Jesus and make way for the kingdom of God.

But there is a second "*Ephphatha!*" that must remove the snares of our nature, the foibles that make us erring, earthbound, and unhappy. Only then are we able to receive eyes that truly see God, only then will we become the way we really want to be, only then will the things of the past cease to weigh us down—those things that cause us to forget that we want to belong to God. We are still broken and bound because we have not heeded this "*Ephphatha!*" which frees us from bondage to the demonic. Even the healthiest people can behave like demons. We haggle and quarrel and do this or that in spite of not wanting to. We find it difficult to put up with each other, we make life complicated, we don't understand each other, and we get angry in spite of not wanting to. We need to pray for the "*Ephphatha!*" that frees us from all these ties.

When we can experience this, we will then hear "*Ephphatha!*" a third time, which frees us from our physical bonds. In the spiritual darkness surrounding us, death rules and makes us feeble, blind, and sick. But if the second "*Ephphatha!*" has come, then outer miracles will occur of themselves. They easily happen if the Savior touches us with his flesh and blood. But this must not come too soon, for we are often not ready for it. Illness is also an inner bondage, an intensification of the demonic. Nothing is worse than an outer healing without the inner "*Ephphatha!*" The third "*Ephphatha!*" must come, not with a trumpet call, but quietly and reverently. It must remain completely in God's hands so that no human can meddle with it.

Perhaps you have already experienced the first "*Ephphatha!*": Jesus lives! Perhaps even now the second is on the way: Jesus rules and frees you. Be assured that the third "*Ephphatha!*" will come as well, where you will be healed in body, too.

We usually look for happiness through a change in our outer circumstances or through adherence to this or that trend. But what is most important is to become inwardly happy, "blessed." And this does not happen through a change of circumstances but through a person. Jesus, God in person, must touch us in such a way that we each can become truly human. Then we will be able to rise above our circumstances. Even the poor, despite their poverty, can become rich in spirit. The rich, too, will be able to cope with their wealth without being harmed by it. The uneducated will be enlightened, and the educated will no longer look down on those who are not. When we are touched by Jesus each one of us, in his or her own way, will become free to be himself, a unique plant of God. Each person and each nation is a unique and eternal work of God. You are you! Be yourself. When God frees you to be yourself, then you are saved. That is the blessedness we receive when we encounter the living Christ.

We need to be re-educated by and for Jesus Christ. Worldly education is not enough. Even our Christianity has failed to produce a genuine Christian education. We have ceased being disciples. We still value far too much the wise and the strong, those who get recognized and honored and hold power. That is what the world prizes. But the kingdom of heaven is approaching, and in this kingdom we will not be taught by human beings, but by God himself. Blessed are the poor and the hungry! Has God chosen the wise? No, he has chosen the lowly, the miserable, all the little creatures whom the world supposes to have been rejected by God.

⊹

Up till now civilization has depended on the sacrifice of human life. How many millions slave away and spend their lives in poverty so that we can enjoy life's advantages? Everything we do is done at the cost of others. In fact, our whole civilized life grinds others to death.

But Jesus came to the miserable and the lost, to those as good as dead, and cared for them. He did so because he wants to bring about a new way, a new culture. Look at Jesus, born in a manger in Bethlehem, Jesus, who proclaims good news to the poor, who continues to come to the needy and the sick and help them. Look at Jesus, the one who feeds the crowds in the desert and cares for the people without a shepherd—look at Jesus, and then you come into the light. Through Jesus, the distressed enter into the light of day—the sick, the spiritually bewildered, the despised, all those who have been trampled on in world history. Jesus brings the poor to the surface. Human civilization has to change. Only when we help the masses will things change for the better. People who gather around Jesus emanate freedom and life, spirit, truth and strength for the poor.

⊹

Jesus wants to lever up the world, not press it down.

⊹

The Father's love touches the very worst of humankind. Everything bound up in sin will be rescued and set free. If a mason wants to lift a stone, he doesn't get hold of the sand that lies on top. He grasps it at the bottom. And when the Father in heaven lifts up humankind *en masse*—weighed down as it is with sin and death—and brings it into the kingdom of God, he cannot possibly skim the good from the top and leave the rest, otherwise the whole lump remains where it is. Jesus takes hold of sinners. He goes to the bottom, where the worst are. It is for this purpose and this purpose alone that he exercises the mighty lifting power of God.

Each one of us must be saved at his or her worst points, too. Everyone has a sordid side, and it is this side that Jesus wants to get at. We must not try to hide it. Jesus has to get hold of what is most corrupt in us in order for him to truly free us. Then we may become joyful children of God.

⟜

Since the time of the apostles, a great battle has been taking place on earth. It is the struggle of enslaved people for their freedom, for their life. When we speak of life, we can only do so when the innumerable chains that bind us are loosed, the bonds, in which most people are languishing. This fight for freedom and life is more active than ever. All the more, we need to raise the banner of the downtrodden and preach good news to the poor. The poor are coming into the light of day. Their history has been quite hidden by the stories of the great and powerful. But new movements toward humanitarianism are emerging. This striving for freedom is a sign of the times, evidence that God's kingdom is on the move.

We must learn again to follow where Jesus goes, who aids the oppressed and needy. For in Jesus, deliverance and redemption of the poor has taken on earthly form. The spirit of truth and justice lives in humanity, and thus repeatedly surfaces. Despite this, it is difficult to make headway against the world spirit, the "spirit of the beast." Even good people, as soon as they attain position and respect, become hardened toward their fellow human beings. The question before us is: Which spirit is master? The spirit of this world or the Spirit of Christ?

At some point, this very question will cause a crisis. Everyone who acknowledges the Spirit of Christ must first experience this crisis within himself as did Paul, who rejected the "spirit of the beast." But once we have fought through this battle within ourselves, we need to remain ever clear-sighted. We must never try to force Christ onto others, especially by violence; it is a crime to associate the sword with the Spirit of Christ. Jesus is gentle and meek, and those who serve him do so in gentleness and meekness.

⟜

When Jesus came into the world he brought judgment. Salvation, yes. But also judgment. He judges sin and in so doing saves the sinner and sets him free from the ravages of sin. He judges the darkness, that is, puts an end to it, but allows that which is truly of God in us to live; yes, through the cross he even cancels the verdict of damnation and delivers the damned. That is the light and the love of God in Christ. It is on this we must be grounded.

⤗

There are two kinds of judgment. One locks the sinner in with his sins, like our prisons do. That is the judgment of wrath, of outrage against the sinner. Jesus' judgment, however, separates the sinner from his sins. This kind of judgment is redemptive. Jesus frees us from our sins and from every condemnation. Who will condemn? God is here who makes us righteous. Now Christ is here, the one who has everything in his hands. He died and rose for us, so that we might receive the seal of a completely new existence. Even in death, the moment we have fellowship with Jesus Christ we can be certain that God's judgment leads to redemption.

It is so painful to see how the enemy has succeeded in arousing so much fear around the subjects of death and judgment, even among those who believe. Yet, let us not forget that wherever Jesus' name is called upon light must dawn. Those who believe in him no longer have to fear judgment. They have fought their way from death to life. May the Father in heaven grant us to see the light of his love, so that we may experience the healing judgment of redemption.

⤗

Jesus must be the first and the only one for us—not just in words but in deeds. Innumerable other sovereignties contend for our allegiance. Sadly, even in our different religious circles, people who profess Jesus allow themselves to be under the sway of completely different authorities. This is why there exist so many divisions among Christians. Already in the apostles' time, there was the danger of becoming a follower of Paul, of Apollos, of Cephas, and not of Jesus alone. Today we say we are Catholic, Protestant, Lutheran, or Calvinist. All the while, love for the Savior disappears. Whenever another authority or name captivates us, genuine dedication to the Savior is lost, and the tremendous, light-giving declaration, "He alone is our king—the one who proceeds from God," is clouded over. We grow degenerate and end up with a Christianity that takes all sorts of human ingenuity to maintain and uses all kinds of worldly means to propagate itself: passion, anger, coercion and pressure, judgment.

The Savior warned his disciples that it would be difficult once he was gone. "Remain in my love," he told them, and then he instituted the Lord's Supper, intending that he would always be honored there as the one and only true bread of life. But it is just here, with this meal, where Jesus alone is to be worshiped, where all egoistic thoughts of self-importance are to cease before his living presence, where he alone is supposed to speak—just here in connection with this most sacred meal that the most divisive doctrines and dogmas have arisen!

We must again learn to cry out: "Jesus!" But we must cry out for Jesus and no one else. Yes, many people preach Jesus. But they preach only a pietistic Jesus. Others, who are attached to some kind of church or tradition, want only a Jesus that suits their own theological ideas. Our human wishes and thoughts far too often count more than Jesus himself. Hence, our plea "Jesus!" no longer has any real power.

In Möttlingen, in 1842, my father was in deep despair. Suddenly all his Christian theories fell by the wayside, and he cried out to Jesus himself. When that happened all his sacred theology was thrown aside. From then on, hardly anyone understood him. I, too, have been misunderstood. Only a silent few have had a presentiment of Jesus *as he is* and have then tried to follow him. When Jesus comes, miracles happen. Something unspeakably great and holy flashes down from heaven—no noise, no violence, no theology. The love of God descends and breaks in with tremendous strength.

When Christianity is popular, it lacks substance. It takes on the character of a religion, comparable to other religions. But Jesus did not bring a better religion—he brought himself, his person. Jesus Christ, yesterday and today and the same in all eternity.

Everything centers on this one question: "Is Jesus Lord or not?" Everything else, religion and Christianity included, is beside the point.

Unfortunately the church has not allowed the one Spirit to rule in its midst, the Spirit that makes all members subject to Jesus Christ. Oh, we work hard—for our own church, our own denomination or sect, our own brand of theology, our own vision of what the world should become—but scarcely do we give a thought to Jesus as the living Lord. It is something tremendous, however, when even two or three become one in his name. Only when the core is genuine will the kingdom of God come.

Therefore let us pray again and again, "Give us the Spirit that enables us to deny ourselves, so that we no longer desire anything for ourselves but instead stand up for Jesus alone—like soldiers for their king—so that he alone is Lord in us and in the world."

That is the goal: Jesus, the Lord ruling upon earth; Jesus, the King of kings; Jesus, the Lord in politics; Jesus, the Lord in our society; Jesus, the Lord in our families; Jesus, the Lord in our customs and traditions; Jesus, the Lord! No laws or human institutions, nothing else, however holy it seems, except Jesus, the Lord, to the honor of God the Father.

# 4

# Our Savior King

A KING CANNOT RULE *as a king* unless the people acknowledge him as one. A king is truly king once the people give him their affection. Jesus is our king, but only when we give him our hearts. He needs to have a people who stand on guard, watching day and night, standing before God the Father, exclaiming, "You sent Jesus to be Lord. You gave him a name above all names. You crowned him with praise and honor. You brought him out of death and made him to be our shepherd. You have shown us that Jesus Christ is Lord, the all-powerful One. That is why we hold high the banner of our king. You sent him to be king, and we need him to become our king."

God's small flock must focus on this one thing—that Jesus is the victorious Lord in every area of life; he rules over all things and must therefore receive the honor due him as king.

⊹

To worship someone is to make him lord.

⊹

Jesus is king—not *a* king, but *the* king—the king of God's grace. Today, however, we have a Christian religion where Christ is but a figurehead. Christ is accepted as part of the bargain of belief, but not in the way that moves us to cry out, "The king is here!" When you are face to face with a king, you have to choose; friend or foe. The same goes with Jesus.

Recall what Peter said to the Jews—he referred to Jesus as the Messiah they crucified (Acts 2:23). People were looking for a savior, nevertheless they crucified God's anointed one, the Christ, the king. This is because what Jesus taught was God's will, which was contrary to their own. We, too, are guilty of crucifying Christ, for he has been crucified throughout the centuries. We have created a false, easy-going Christianity in which we have set things up to satisfy our own longings, not God's.

Why don't we stand up for Jesus? Jesus wants to have disciples who renounce everything and commit everything to him, the king. Christ is Lord and it is to his authority alone we are to bow—not the government, not the church of Protestantism or Catholicism, not even the teachings of Christ as you or I conceive them. Our king is Christ himself; we are called to submit to the will of God in Christ alone.

We can falsely worship Christ. In fact, thousands of Christians worship the Savior in much the same way pagans worship their gods. They worship Christ to satisfy their own wishes. They only preoccupy themselves with God's help in terms of what he can do for them. This is nothing but blasphemy. Whether we are poor, sick, or unhappy Jesus says, "Come with me, and I will lead you to my Father and to his will. First come with me to God, then you will have everything you need. I don't want or need your flattery. I want your whole being."

Following Jesus demands a fight unto death—a death to our own wills and a death to all that stands in the way of our ultimate allegiance to him. We need a church that is entirely under the cross of Jesus, free from all worldly atmospheres, one that radiates light and is salt for the world. May God grant that the guilt of many centuries is blotted out: that our own self-love is crucified.

✢

Jesus Christ has been crowned the Savior and sits on the throne of God. It is the crowned Savior in heaven, the Alpha and Omega, who is Lord over history. Redemption will come only from him—both to us and to the whole world.

This Christ was "crowned" three times—when he died, when he arose, and when he sat down at the right hand of the Father in heaven. He will not relinquish anything, be it his death, his resurrection, or his future throne. This is his promise to us. He holds in his hands our past, our present, and our future.

Christ will always be the Lamb who bleeds, who washes away our sins and the sins of the world. His death redeems our past. Our sins, whatever they happen to be and however far back they were committed, must vanish. When you don't know what to do in the face of your sin, think of the crown of Christ's death. Do not trash yourself. Do not despair. Know that Jesus died and that he carries your every sin. Everything depends on this; the bleeding Savior and his victory on the cross (not our past nor our sin) is final.

But there is more. Because Christ arose, he offers life to everyone, both to the dead and to the living. He speaks to us today, even while we are surrounded by the forces of death. He rises from the grave; yes, he is risen and henceforth wipes away the powers of death from our lives. He wears the crown of his resurrection *today*. His resurrection is not just a miraculous occurrence of the past we can read about in a book. It is a fact here and now and can be applied to our own lives today. We have a Savior now. He lives. He is here. Feel his power; it can free you not only from sin, but from the fear of death itself.

Christ wears yet another crown: the crown of his life in God's future. Why do we experience so little when it comes to his death and resurrection? It is because we have neglected to consider the future of Jesus Christ. The fact that Jesus is sitting at the right hand of the Father in heaven has unbelievable power for the future. It is this future that transforms us inwardly. Jesus Christ, yesterday, today, and also the same in eternity. Or do you think that the Savior admonishes us for no reason when he says, "Wait, until I come" (Matt 24:42)? Do you think his cause will be completed on earth without him having a say in the matter? The only way we can be his servants and his disciples is when we have *him* as he will be with us. The Lord Jesus will not relinquish the crown of his future. He *will* come, even if there are only five wise virgins waiting for him.

⟜⟝

When Jesus says, "All authority in heaven and on earth has been given to me" (Matt 28:18), he means to say that he is the one whom God Almighty has given to all creation. He holds the universe in his hands, like a king who rules his kingdom firmly and leads it to what is good. These words of Jesus are like a ladder on which we can ascend into God's world. Hence, we can say to the whole of creation, "Be comforted. There exists a supreme authority, and that authority is coming, and it will put everything in order." This is the good news of Jesus Christ, "The nations are mine, and in my name you should raise the banner of God the Father over all nations to God's honor. The nations are mine, and you are to baptize them in my authority so that they might become true people. The nations are mine, therefore lead them right where heaven opens, right where the ruler comes—the one who has authority in heaven and on earth" (Matt 28:19–20).

Jesus is faithful, and he continues to be Christ right up to the present day. The burden falls on us—we have not been faithful. We have failed to recognize the indescribable mercy of God and thus don't cherish it in our hearts. From heaven we are flooded with warmth and constant attention, but on earth we remain cold. Yet God is faithful—even the judgments he sends upon us are signs of his goodness. He does not want to let us go. He will not allow us simply to perish. Though the earth is cold and dead, heaven is warm and living. And one day the warmth of life will conquer earth.

What does God want? He wants us to give him our whole hearts, our undivided allegiance to his kingdom. He wants us to be gripped by one thing: the majesty of God and his reign. "Jesus is king to the glory of God, the Father in heaven." That is what is most important. Be on guard against losing this reverence for God, which can so easily get lost in all our studying and in all our theology. Today people think they are achieving a lot by elaborating all their theological ideas, by writing more books, and by developing more religious schemes. All the while God's kingdom gets clouded over. All our scholarly and spiritual achievements are useless. Once reverence for God and respect for Jesus as God's appointed prince on earth cease to be firmly rooted in our hearts, then all we are left with is a human democracy in which people are free to give their heart to whomever or whatever he or she likes.

The "waters" of modern Christianity are so muddied precisely because we each do whatever we like. We pursue God's kingdom by our own wits. Oh, there are plenty of guerilla fighters, but they all run around with no commander. Therefore, what we see today is not God's kingdom, not Christ's victory over the devil, but the victory of sin and death. They, not God, are taking over. Only Christ can rescue us!

But Jesus needs believers with undivided hearts: diverse bands of individuals who will join hands and rejoice together in service to the one Lord. Somewhere there has to be a people, a family of God in the world, who serve him unreservedly. God's kingdom can never come as long as we are inattentive and scattered, if all we do is direct our wills in different directions. We must listen to *one* commander together and do his bidding.

Unbelievers rightly condemn Christianity because what they see is clearly not what Christ our Savior came to bring. So we have to wake up. Let the Savior be king! He is the majesty. God is love and he will always be love, but if we profess this God and then run after other gods or give ourselves to lesser things; if we can't free ourselves from father or mother, wife or child, church or denomination, people or country, ideology or theology; if we can't say, "Jesus alone!" and *live* accordingly, then we will not receive the blessings of God's kingdom. Therefore, let us fight loyally for the one King, and let us do so zealously, with all our heart, soul, strength, and mind.

We don't need another "confession" about Jesus Christ. *We need him.* In the Gospels we find no confession, except this: Jesus is Lord! No, Jesus himself is at the center, always and only, Jesus. We have let far too much come between him and us. Now put him first.

"You are from below," the Savior said. In other words, we are historical people, an earthly people. "But I am from above" (John 8:23). Jesus is free from father and mother, temple and nation, and traditions. When he came to earth it was God himself, not man, who prepared the way. Therefore he says, "Follow me! Whoever acknowledges me—the eternal one, the one who lives among you without traditions, the one who disregards your piety and your righteousness and inquires only for God—I will acknowledge before my Father in heaven (Matt 10:32). But those who preoccupy themselves with what is from below, who look at life from the vantage point of family and state and nation and church, they do not acknowledge me, and thus I will not acknowledge them."

If the children of God are silent, "the stones must cry out." We need a violent shock. Only then can Jesus Christ come again to this world—Jesus, this free man, this simple man of God, this Son of Man. He wants us, too, to be born from above. But if we Christians are content to be like everyone else, then why bother about being Christian at all? Our calling is to bring the "stream" of God to earth, that pure stream from above that seeks to flood the world. Unless we do this, we will rot away. But no! Jesus commands us to bring forth fruit that will last—Jesus, the free Jesus, God's Son, the free man, the only one begotten of God, the Savior of the world.

❧

Perhaps one of the greatest misfortunes on earth is that there are Christians without Christ, disciples without the Master. Many people want to follow Christ, but they won't let go; they won't surrender their entire lives to him, including all their good ideas. And so they grab for and chase after other lights. They run to others crying out, "Help me, do whatever you can to help!" With that, the very rope that connects them to Jesus breaks.

❧

A time will come when no one will be allowed to say, "I belong to Jesus," unless he lives like Jesus did (1 John 2:6). No longer will people be able to govern or preach in the name of Christ and at the same time quarrel, fight, and spill blood. A new time is coming.

❧

As a true wife is "hidden" in her husband, we must be "in Christ." A devoted wife not only senses her husband's wishes in practical matters, she knows his inner longings. She notices, without having to be told, what her husband wants. She is aware of his unspoken needs. It is something like this when we are "in Jesus." We are aware of what he wants. We live in him and he in us.

❧

The Savior says, "Unless you eat the flesh of the Son of Man and drink his blood, you have no life in you" (John 5:53). Our life depends on all sorts of eating. Every breath is an intake of nourishment. Every refreshing experience is nourishment. Any physical or spiritual activity can nourish us. Even sleep refreshes us. If, however, poison gets into our food, we suffer.

The same can happen to us spiritually. Today people eat all kinds of bad things spiritually. Good Christians feed themselves on a vast array of religious education, consuming an enormous amount of spiritual knowledge. Yet, you can't even talk sensibly with them because of what they have "fed" themselves on. One person will read a book, another will study a famous personality or saint, another will devour this or that new idea. But all this leads to human splendor, and in the end brings them to a dead end. All this "spiritual learning" is still only "bread"—nourishment that comes from flesh and blood.

Jesus alone is the bread of life. "Whoever eats this bread—whoever eats my flesh and drinks my blood—will have eternal life" (John 7:51–56). Only he is able to provide inner nourishment, yet only if we have an inner connection to him. He lives, and so we can take him into ourselves and be formed by him. Our body, soul, and spirit must be shaped by him. Let this kind of training override all other forms of education.

Truth cannot live unless someone is willing to represent it. Therefore, we who believe in Christ must actively show who Jesus is.

# 5

## God's People

AT THE TIME WHEN Christ appeared, God's people were waiting for God's kingdom. That is the reason why the world was ready for harvesting.

✧

We will never be able to advance God's kingdom with books or speeches or elaborate explanations. We have to be people who live in the light of Jesus Christ and in his strength. Only then will this dark world grow light. That is why it says, "Arise, shine!" (Isa 60:1). It does not say, "Write books," but, "Shine! Be a light!"

✧

God's light enters our world by shining through people. We, however, insist on looking for the light in books; we seek for it in opinions, doctrines, and human constructs. But a person can have an interesting viewpoint and still be living in sin; they can use fine words but still possess a coarse inner life. We must learn again that the light of God is found not in concepts, but in people.

Yet even here there is the great danger of being misled. Satan also casts a "light" on people. He too is an angel of "light." He knows full well that the true light comes upon people and therefore schemes by casting his "light" on people. Thus we hear from many different voices, "It is me!" and thousands echo, "It is him!"

It can be very difficult to differentiate the true light from all the false lights that grab our attention, and this is because the latter usually appear in the name of Jesus Christ. But mark this: those who rule by force, who dictate commands, and coerce people into submission have nothing to do with the true light. Like the sun, God's light enables a person to shine brightly. The light that comes from Jesus makes people shine and frees them from themselves. But whenever people feel embarrassed or ashamed, whenever they are frightened, whenever they lack peace—they are in darkness, not light. Only when people feel revived, when they are at ease, when they are full of life and strength and can endure grief, when they can look at corruption and still have hope, when they soar on wings like eagles (Isa 40:31) in spite of all their misery—this is the mark of genuine light. When violence ceases, when freedom exists from within, when God's love lives, the love that embraces the sinner, the love that despises no one and is even concerned for the enemy's welfare—this is the true light of Jesus Christ.

⊷

In Isaiah, God's servant despairs: "I have labored in vain; I have spent my strength for nothing" (Isa 49:4). But God assures him and promises to protect him, for his servant will be "a covenant for the people to restore the land" (Isa 49:8).

We look back with pride on the fruits of our labor and point to the works of our hands, our intellect, and our organizational talents. With all our achievements, however, little or nothing is gained for the improvement of humanity. The servant of God, however, relies on God's strength, not his own. He cannot point to any achievement of his own. Nonetheless, he is the very one God protects and makes to be a covenant for the people.

Christ is God's true servant; he is the power and love of God for all people. Without him we are severed from God and his righteousness. Only through him and through his power can we be redeemed. But Jesus did not create an organization, he did not set up any political, social, or ecclesiastical structure; he did not establish any institution. He lived right alongside us. He dwelt in our midst and worked amongst us. He did not "stir hand or foot" to change anything—not against the Romans or against the Temple.

No, he was *the* man from whom streamed the hope that would set the world right and set people free.

This Jesus, though no longer visible here on earth, continues to work—through his apostles and his servants. In fact, a continuous stream of servant figures has flowed from Jesus right through history. Granted, it appears to us that they have also worked in vain. Other people have founded churches and large institutions, they have put themselves forward politically and socially: "Look at our institutions, our churches, our schools, our splendid organizations!" But God's servant knows that these things cannot restore us. More importantly, he can yet represent Jesus and make visible his ongoing work of restoring the human race. The servant of God who holds firmly to him will win the victory. His faith will overcome the spirit of this age. Renewal will come; Paradise, our original home, *will* be restored.

❧

Again and again God needs a people for Zion. Zion is not a place, but a kingly realm in which God's Spirit rules. But Zion, by itself, remains unfruitful as long as it has no people. God needs people who are partners with him. The number of Zion's people is unimportant—it's the quality that counts. God's people must be priestly people, with hearts courageous enough to take on the burden of the whole world. They must be people who don't deliberate or question too much, but who trustingly look to the Father in heaven. They aren't philosophers, they aren't wise or clever, but they do have great longings and sturdy souls. They experience the sorrows of the world, while praising God and working for Zion day after day.

Zion is famished for such people. Zion—where the Spirit reigns on God's throne—is splendidly prepared to exercise its rule, but this Spirit needs people, true men and women, not half-hearted imitators. Maybe you feel like you already are such a person, but also realize that you need to show it more in deeds. Just know that if you are called to Zion, you must be unshakable, convinced to the bone, otherwise you will not be "harnessed to the cart." And God will not harness up just anyone. Harnessing someone up who then makes the cart get stuck is far worse than adding no one. As soon as God harnesses someone up to the cart, be assured that new life comes on earth. The world as we know it is judged, and begins to fade away.

When God's kingdom comes, watch out—your hair will stand on end. You will have to tear out of your heart all your favorite ideas. There will be no time for bargaining. God will not have any more patience. At last the decks will be cleared. You may even have to go through slime and filth, fire and water. For when God makes his arrival, he comes to be your king. The day is drawing near for Zion's people, people who are rock solid. God will not allow his kingdom to be undermined forever. A great light will one day be lit and nations which are groaning for redemption will rejoice.

⊹

"When you pass through the rivers, they will not sweep over you. When you walk through the fire, you will not be burned" (Isa 43:2). So writes Isaiah. But this promise is not for everyone. Many people perish in their misery—both physically and spiritually. Yet, there are always a few who have a special protection. The Bible calls them "servants of God." They encounter the same dangers as others, but instead of perishing, instead of being wounded, they are strengthened. To them God says, "You are mine," and if we hold firmly to his call, we are under God's protection.

God protects all those who understand that there is no greater happiness than serving God. But, if serving God is not our highest priority, we will not experience the miracles that are promised to God's servants. Nothing is worse than halfhearted godliness, than being lukewarm, than living merely on the side. God cannot stomach such a life. Those who are lukewarm are warned that they will be spat out—rejected from God's kingdom and from working for God's kingdom.

God's call is simple. When he beckons to us, we become his possession: "You are mine." God's call can come to anyone—to a master or a servant, to a preacher in the pulpit or a child at his play. It's not a matter of becoming someone you are not. A king may remain a king; a laborer may continue doing his job. You do not have to become a preacher or a missionary in order to heed God's call. God's ultimate will is the same for everyone. So riches can't harm you. Neither can poverty. In whatever state you are in, the call is that you become a true person. The word of God makes you genuine. Anything that is false about you will vanish as soon as you sincerely accept the word of God. Simply be happy and childlike. Your life is now God's. From now on you are under his protection and you will experience the same miracles as Abraham did.

⊹

When a servant of God dies in the complete steadfastness of an undivided will, the seeds of his life will sprout after his death.

＋

God has chosen us in Jesus Christ. Let this realization make you strong. When a storm is raging in your heart, when your emotions are all riled up, when sin and folly overwhelm you, when death has you in its clutches— then know that sin does not have you, neither does death. You are *in* Christ. God alone has you. The Savior has chosen you, and since you have been chosen, it is not just a matter of becoming "devout"—no! You have entered God's kingdom, the region where God rules, removed from the powers of this world, removed from your own powers, and given over into the glorious and glorifying power of God.

Don't ever think that God has chosen others, but not you. In God's kingdom things are not so tidy or "logical." God's love is meant for every person who comes to Jesus. Anyone who is called is therefore also chosen. Believe then that you are chosen. If you have a longing for God, where do you think that longing comes from? And even if you have to go through hell, even if your heart shivers and shakes with fear, you are still chosen. You may sink into the depths, but you will rise again to the heights. God has chosen you. You are *his,* and no one else's.

＋

God must always have people, those whom he has chosen, who allow themselves and the things they have to be used for others. Many people are afraid of the idea of someone being chosen. They can't imagine that someone can have a position without dominating. But it should be different among God's people. God lives, but his life is always for others. All the creatures are his, and we know this because it is he who feeds them all. God's chosen ones are meant to be godly, but they are godly only because they help others, they share their possessions with them and carry their burdens.

＋

God is not content with saving just a few individuals. He looks beyond the few to the many—to *all* who are lost. Abraham was not called or granted peace at the expense of the world. On the contrary, Abraham suffered *for* the world. It was at Abraham's expense that God looked upon the nations. Israel was chosen so that God could reveal himself to all nations, to the vast host of humanity—all God's sheep. At Israel's expense, God reaches out to all people, and at Jesus' expense, too, God reaches out to the whole world. Yes, at the expense of Jesus' church, the world is to be blessed.

So we must offer ourselves. We are God's reinforcements, so to speak, to help him look for his sheep. Sadly, there do not seem to be enough people at whose expense God can work. We are much too selfish, especially with all our Christianity. We only turn to God for our own gain, and hence lack the real fighting strength to be of any use. We vacillate and thus God cannot depend on us. How can this be? Thousands die for their country, so why aren't we Christians ready to die for our faith, for the will of God, who is the Father of all people? Why are we so selfish and halfhearted? We gladly do favors for others but only as long as they don't interfere with our comfortable lives. What's wrong with us? Why aren't we enthusiastic for the cause of God, for finding God's sheep—all the humble and poverty-stricken ones? Why are we so unwilling to give ourselves entirely to God? Why are we so consumed with what might happen to us? There must be some people, somewhere, who are ready to expend themselves for God's cause.

People claim the blood of Jesus Christ for their own blessedness. But what the blood of Christ actually demands is that we sacrifice our very lives. Then God's kingdom will come.

The apostles did not "instruct" us about dogma, but gave us guidelines on how to follow Jesus. They taught us from the battlefield. Their instructions were given to us, Jesus' disciples, not to the masses. Orders given to officers and soldiers do not concern the public. Likewise, Jesus' teachings cannot simply be applied to the whole of humankind. This would be demanding too much. Nevertheless, we do have a message for the masses. The gospel is quite simple: "Fear God and honor him. Stay where you are and live for God. His grace has been given to you. Light will come. Be comforted." The gospel does not govern like a parliament. Rather, it says, "Be assured that the cause is in good hands. We have a great King, who will accomplish his rule for all people. You belong to God." It is this simple realization that must penetrate the masses. "You belong to God. No one will fall from his hands."

Christians are too cowardly to proclaim their faith. This is because we expect too much of people. We must begin with this simple message and proclaim, "You belong to God, and you will not fall from his hands." So let us not think that some people belong to God and others don't. Is this progress, a sign of God's new work? Progress lies in taking hold of the whole world even though it has grown alien to God through sin. "They are mine," God says. He has sent his Son, and this is what brings the healing grace of God to all human beings.

↶

From the great mass of all people, God calls out a little flock for his ministry. He delivers this flock from all unrighteousness and makes it *his* possession. He equips it with wisdom and strength to defend his cause on earth—for the benefit of all, not against or in judgment on anyone. His flock has the ministry to intercede for all people. They hold on to the gospel, "From today on, everything and everyone belongs to God!"

↶

"No one can say, 'Jesus is Lord,' except by the Holy Spirit" (1 Cor 12:2). If people are not *able* to, then they also cannot be condemned. They are not yet complete—they still belong to the wretched ones.

↶

The fact that Jesus sent his disciples into the world opens up a new world. God's world fights against the old order that we are so accustomed to. Yes, this world has existed for thousands of years. The light of God's eternal reign has even shone upon it. Nevertheless, it is buried in lies. Even Israel, God's nation, has been smothered over with deception. Just like the high waves of a storm breaking on the shore, human opinions and lies have "crashed" over Israel.

But in Jesus, and through his followers, God's world begins anew. God builds around himself a fortress of love against which the surging waves of this dark world cannot prevail. This fortress will never fall. Jesus is there! When Jesus was on earth the atmosphere of God's kingdom camped round about him and protected him. Storms among the nations, both of an outer and inner nature, wars and bloodbaths, satanic currents in human thought—all of these wanted to remove Jesus, the Lord, out of their way. But they could not. And even today they cannot overpower him or the believers who stand at his side.

⌖

We should be thankful for the advances brought about by teachers, scientists, medical doctors, and philanthropists. But all these are one-sided. What do we gain by having a civilization that turns its back on God?

⌖

Whoever has the "crown of life" really has something. But people today make all kinds of crowns for themselves, accomplishments that consist of insignificant matters. They will surely lose them. For example, even now military men are losing their "crowns" because today we long for heroes of peace, not war. Crowns in the sciences or the arts also fade. But for those who stand up for God and for the life in God that we will all one day take part in—they will receive a crown that lasts forever. The life and testimony of a man of God will never fade away. Alexander the Great and other "greats" of this world will lose their crowns. But Moses will not, nor Isaiah, nor Peter.

So let us work for the *highest* advances for humanity, advances of an inner nature. Let us give witness to a new kind of education. If we are faithful in this, we will receive a crown of life and also have something worth saying.

⌖

The kingdom of God will not strike like a catastrophe. It will come gradually. The world is not evil in itself. Rather it is like raw material and therefore must be cultivated by God himself through his Spirit. For this to happen, God uses people who can speak a decisive word about life.

⊷

Jesus is the light of the world. One could also say he is the educator of the world. Since Jesus lives solely from God, he knows how to talk and relate to everyone, even the godless. This is why God's people must first and foremost be educated in *life*. The Greeks were educated in the arts and the sciences; the Romans in government. Neither, however, knew of the kind of life that really satisfies. God's people need to understand life—not just the life of the individual but also the life of brotherhood and community. They should know why we are on this earth, and what is right and true. In Christ, life on earth, creation itself, takes on a new character, new meaning.

Today, however, there are millions of "Christians" who are as clueless about life's meaning as the rest. Countless numbers expend their energies preparing for the next world, but fail to exhibit God's light in this one. They are bereft of "the virtues of God, who calls them into his wonderful light" (1 Pet 2:9). What we need are Christians who put on the virtues of God. The world is not asking, "What do you believe?" but, "How do you live?" They are seeking to find another way in this life.

Our task is to find God's way in everything, including how to earn a living, in buying and selling, in all the work we do. It is possible to not be tied to every penny or chained like slaves to any job. We should help others become free, so that no one is exploited. For, the most miserable and downtrodden and all who are oppressed are God's people, too. We need to help each person develop freely so that they can fit into God's plan for this earth. Every person is called to be a miniature reflection of God. The time will come when we will look for happiness where it can truly be found: in the virtues of God found in daily life.

⊷

It is not in our power to become truly human. For this we need strength from Jesus. That is what the followers of Christ must devote themselves to. The church consists of people through whom the powers of God are revealed. His people renounce all human capabilities. Their God is their strength. Even if they are attacked on all sides, "hard pressed," through

God's strength they will not be overwhelmed. God's people may, like everyone else, be attacked by fear, but they do not despair. They carry Christ's seal, so that the resurrection can be seen in them. They suffer, but only so that a greater, boundless power can enter this world. The resurrection continues; it lives on through all people who follow Christ completely.

⌁

We must be an expectant church, a church that sees to it that heavenly powers flow into the world. Because we wait for God's final kingdom, we are doorkeepers. We are not called to do great things—no, rather to small deeds of service for our Lord. We fulfill our calling just by standing at the door being doorkeepers. And those who are truly watching notice how many doors are indeed being opened. They see how the Savior is already on his way, and they are given into their hearts and souls the clarity of truth. Even in the sorrows and pains of this life, they somehow understand.

As doorkeepers we are glad to wait with patience because we know that the Lord is near. Watching makes time pass quickly. And while we watch, we should pray. Many Christians think it is foolish to pray for the Savior's coming. They say the time of his coming is already set in heaven, so why bother praying? But please allow us to be foolish! As doorkeepers we can't help but pray, "Lord Jesus, come!" We must pray. No one can forbid us from praying for the Lord's coming. No one!

⌁

The gospel announces the arrival of God's kingdom: God is intervening in our human affairs. Even though God's intervention (which happens each day) is not completed, the good news is that his coming kingdom will be consummated.

This new time of God's future begins now for anyone who carries the gospel in their hearts, for anyone who is convinced of the actual arrival of God's reign. The gospel doesn't just talk about a new time—it demonstrates it. It proves that sins are already being forgiven, that people can experience help from above now. The gospel not only proclaims God's coming, it is the power that enables those who proclaim it to live in harmony with it. Believers, companions of Jesus Christ, demonstrate the future of God's kingdom by their actions. With their whole being they vouch for this kingdom. They do not look backwards or sideways, only forwards. And they are certain of this one thing: "Even if we don't know what God's kingdom will finally be like, we know that Jesus is Lord."

⊷

Many people think only about the present, "Eat, drink, and be merry, for tomorrow we die." The Bible calls them "rich" (Luke 6:24; 12:16–21). They indulge in all sorts of pleasures that are easily available and fleeting. Then, when God comes with his food, they have already had their fill. The "poor," however, think about better things, higher things, and finally after striving for these things they realize that help comes only from God. Blessed are these poor, the poor in spirit, for theirs is the kingdom of heaven (Luke 6:20; Matt 5:3).

We need people who are "poor" in this sense, those who cry out as though there were no God on earth. God does not forget the cries of these poor. They are his people on earth. God always sees to it that there are people on earth who are poor, for they alone can be used for the building of God's kingdom. God protects the person of noble soul; he makes sure that their path in life does not lead them toward riches. Unlike superficial Christians, who only want to float on high, they are among God's poor who cry out to God and keep God connected to humankind.

So many Christians today get drunk on the Bible or on religious experiences, but their fervor doesn't last, nor is it genuine. Thank God if you are not one of these rich Christians. If you have to groan and sigh, then groan and sigh in faith and you will be truly rich. Yes, groaning makes you rich. A jovial Christianity does not belong in a world where millions of people live and die in misery, a world ruined by murder, deceit, cruelty, greed, and envy, a world in which nations destroy each other. Our outcry must be passionate. Poor people is what we should be, hungry for God's presence and power, hungry for the coming of the Savior, hungry for the Holy Spirit to be our teacher and guide.

Even the Savior joined ranks with the poor, although he certainly was blessed with all God's gifts. He became the very poorest of the poor, when he cried out, "My God, why have you forsaken me?" (Matt 27:46). This same outcry is our way to God and God's way to us. As long as we rely on other measures—means that only provide temporary relief—we will not receive the necessary power from above to overcome all that is crooked in this world. A mere piece of God's kingdom is not enough; general improvement is of no help. Just a little bit of Christianity, a bit of teaching and preaching, some religious practices here and there, they are all useless. The complete rule of God has to be drawn down to earth. Christ himself must be supreme. Science, technology, "progress" may be very inspiring, but they are not the work of the Holy Spirit. A new world can come only when we ourselves become completely poor. It takes the cry, "Nothing but God," for God's kingdom to advance.

Many people want to bring about a totally new order of society, and they work for it heart and soul. These reformers have high hopes. But what if they succeed, what then? Will a new set of laws help us? No! What we need is for God to be on the throne; we need him to rule more freely in our midst. Once this happens, the outcry of the world's revolutionaries will ultimately serve God, too. When the poor cry out, they do it for the whole world. Their cries will help to draw God's rule down to earth so that ultimately the whole world will not be able to lift a finger except to benefit God's kingdom. There will be a day when the influence of the poor will be far greater than the power of the rich. It is they who will call down the rule of God.

❧

God pours his Spirit into broken vessels.

❧

Who is a true servant of God? It is the one who cries out on account of the misery of the world. The prophets of old took the side of the poverty-stricken. Jesus, too, in a special way, not only in words but with power, became human in order to cry out to God from the lowest and most miserable depths, "My God, my God! Why have you forsaken me?" God's rulership begins with self-denial, and self-denial starts the moment we turn our hearts to the poor, when we walk the lowly path of the Savior.

❧

Jesus gives us more than merely the refreshing of the body, which is destined for the grave. He works toward "that Day," toward God's kingdom of justice and peace. Instead of believing in the Lord of that Day, we are satisfied with just being healthy. But what then of the miracles of God? Don't they point us to the coming of God's reign? Surely God wants to provide us with help, but help that is not just for this earthly life. Let us, therefore, look beyond the present day and to God's future.

⟁

Often times it is difficult to see any justice or righteousness on earth—then we hunger and thirst for it. But it hurts to be hungry. No one can stand being hungry and thirsty for long. In fact, a famished person who sees no hope of food may turn brutal. When there is a lack of justice, people become spiritually dull, abandoning God. Therefore, the reason why there is so much unbelief is often because people are tired of being hungry. Unbelievers are certainly not inhuman. On the contrary, they are often noble. As believers we must pity such unbelievers—they are perishing because of a lack of justice. They see religion and piety—but not justice, and that is why they have lost faith in God.

Most pious people simply don't hunger for justice. In fact, they want to avoid the need for justice altogether. They give the impression of being satisfied, but are actually sorely lacking, and this annoys other people. All of us, however, have to hunger for the justice of God's kingdom. As long as things are not as they should be we must hunger. Only then will the unbelieving look to us, instead of looking down on us. "Come to church—let us hunger together—let us cry together—let us pray together for God's kingdom." That should be our message.

Only Jesus can satisfy our "hunger." But if we want our hunger to be satisfied, we have to be prepared to embrace God's judgment. If you want justice you have to reckon on judgment as part of your commitment. Jesus Christ is already the judge of the living and the dead. If I live for him, I must expect to be judged by him. But his judgment is good for us. And when Jesus appears, we will be even poorer than we are now, because our sin will come fully into the light. When he appears, we will see the evil inside us for what it is. Whatever is not good will be revealed in his light. Though we have been used to turning a "blind eye" on many of our sins, we won't be able to anymore. God's word brings judgment, but it also always brings love. Praise God when filth comes to light. "Lord Jesus, come with your light so that the malice in us will not remain hidden." Only when our fallen condition comes to light can we or anyone else be helped. But first we must "hunger," because only a hungry person can be satisfied. Blessed are you who hunger for justice, because you will be helped (Matt 5:6).

But let us remember that anyone who wants their hunger to be satisfied will also have to open their mouths and chew their food. Our hunger will not be satisfied unless we make some effort. Yes, it is all grace, but it is also grace that we have a mouth to chew our food. If we don't have the energy to feed ourselves, to fight against injustice, if we simply lay back and expect God to do everything, then we will soon sleep the sleep of the unrighteous. Those who seek for God's righteousness do not sleep; they fight with resolute faith, day and night, for what is good. The Savior comes to those who are tireless helpers. We have to work if we want our hunger for justice to be filled. Only then will we see what is possible at the side of the Almighty Savior.

⌀

People from humble circumstances are sometimes our angels. The despised of this earth are actually here to help us. Those who usually don't have much to say can sometimes speak the most important word. Several times God has sent my way a very humble, rejected person, who said something unawares that I needed to hear. My first reaction is usually, "Why should *he* have something to say to me?" But then I realize that I am ignoring the very voice of God. Often God puts someone in our path to prevent an accident, or to sharpen our character. We must always be ready to listen. Many a king has come into great need simply because they would not let their servants speak to them. They were too proud to listen, too vain to take to heart the incidental remark. Oh, that we might learn to listen to and welcome those of humble circumstances.

⌀

God's kingdom will finally be brought about by lowly people, people with no reputation—the despised and rejected. On that Day, the great and strong of this world will come into God's hands as booty when everything is finished. They will learn that God's kingdom is established by poor, simple souls who depend on God's love and on the revelation of God given directly into their hearts.

⊷

As a Christian you cannot achieve anything. You have only to believe and to live out the good news. The Savior takes care of the rest.

⊷

The believers in Jesus Christ are God's temple on earth, and in this temple holiness prevails. It is made up of all those who are faithful to God's truth and heed his authority on earth. Without such a temple, God's kingdom cannot clearly manifest itself. That is why the prophets and the apostles are so zealous for the purity of the temple. How dare we come and sit down in this temple with an unclean heart! How dare we break off the sharp point of God's holy will! In God's temple, people courageously carry out God's will, come what may. They fight with determination within themselves, on themselves, and against themselves. They love the world, but with God's holy love, fighting tooth and nail for Christ's purity wherever they are, so that no other authority can enter into the circle of those who represent God's kingdom on earth.

⊷

The followers of Christ must not allow any false influences to enter their hearts. There is so much today which comes storming in at us, demanding our attention. Science, art, new inventions and ideas, different customs and traditions—they all have their value and place. We don't need to necessarily reject them or the many useful things we have devised. But we must be on guard against and root out the spirit in these things that wants to take over our lives.

⊷

Anyone who embraces Jesus as Lord must strip themselves. Only then are they able to enter God's world of truth. Human goodness is not sufficient. Neither is human brilliance. Jesus needs people who have been completely sanctified for God, entirely submerged into his will. This does not mean leaving the world. No. We have been placed in the world for a purpose: to enter just those places where everything is in conflict. God's love embraces the world and its need, and that's why in the arms of Jesus' disciples the world will be judged; whatever is false will be revealed. All the more, Christ's disciples must not abandon the world. Never! They must love it with the love of God. He wants the world to die, come to an end, so that it might become brand new.

✢

Just having the same views about the Bible, God, and Christ does not make us a united people of God. We will be God's people only when we occupy ourselves with God, not ourselves and our ideas. God is interested in us, but not in the way we think. Christ came to forgive our sins and make us blessed, but he also came to look for a firm, fighting band that stands totally for God, faithfully giving themselves to win the world for God.

✢

There are dear, good Christians (who certainly will receive a little spot in heaven), but who don't have a minute free to work for God. My, they have a lot of requests on their hearts! They want to be healthy, or rich, or happy, or stay with father and mother. They seek to be forgiven for their many sins. But they are not really aware of the kingdom of God. They live in a mishmash that consists of both temporal and eternal life. Jesus is their Master at one moment and something else the next. They follow him one minute but then go their own way the next. If we really want to be disciples of Jesus, it will cost us our lives.

✢

We need not fear evil, *per se*, but evil mixed with truth. That's when things get dangerous. The serpent in Paradise spoke as if it had come from God. His tactics were sly and cunning. The most dangerous spirits are the ones who want to do their own "good" works, but not God's. They wander away from God and his way. Herein lay the source of temptation. A whole culture can arise that looks good, but all the while "glues our eyes shut" so we cannot recognize God's genuine creation. It blocks our ears from hearing the true word of God. Such a culture sinks into us in such a way that even noble and honest people say, "We cannot understand God. We don't know what you are talking about." Although many people feel the need for religion, they are blinded by their surrounding culture. We have to pray that God will open our eyes and ears so that we will receive again the word of God. Then we can learn to distinguish between the original and the counterfeit. Only then will we be able to offer a genuine word of God to those who hunger for it.

⋄

When we hear what Jesus expects of us, we might think to ourselves, "I can't do that. No one could do that!" That's true. No one can! That is why we have to become completely different people.

⋄

The spirit of this world has wormed its way into the church, and thus the church has almost lost the fight against the demons of darkness and deception. There will never be a *real* victory for God's kingdom until a decision is made within the church: "Who is Lord? Jesus or the world?"

The answer to this question comes from within. There is a fight that takes place within each one of us. It is as though two spirits live in us; one that longs for God and another that serves selfish desires. Thank God if you feel this fight in your heart. It will go well for you the moment you take up the battle against the flesh and its desires. Jesus will win the victory; he will conquer in you all that opposes God. But more than that, he will go on to conquer all that has wormed its way into the church, and from there he will conquer the world. His light will dawn everywhere—in the visible and invisible world, upon the dead and the living.

⋄

Among Jesus' closest circle, it was Judas—Jesus' betrayer—who held the money bag. What should the Savior have done about this? Why didn't he just knock the money bag out of Judas's hand? Because Judas had to knock the bag out of his own hands! The Savior never raises his fist. Instead, he allows things to take their course. People knock down, dismiss, or trash others—any king can do that. But the Savior does not do this. Thank and praise God that the Savior does not get rid of obstacles by force. He is our Savior, not our hero. He came to save sinners, not destroy them. Even Judas, Jesus did not reject him; on his side he did not let the "thread" between them break. Even after being betrayed, Jesus carried Judas in love. If Judas was eternally lost, as people think, Jesus would have thrust him away from himself. But he didn't. Jesus remains Judas's king and Savior.

The followers of Jesus Christ are supposed to be one people, united under one king. But this is seldom the case. We see this person over there or that person here serving God, but as soon as there are several together, they turn away from the Lord and start looking at each other in envy and jealousy. They become consumed with themselves and their own gifts and callings. Despite good intentions, separation occurs, which over time only gets worse and worse. Then different traditions develop, which eventually get treated as being part of the Christian faith itself. All this is very sad.

It is a tremendous blessing, therefore, whenever God puts the Savior back into the center as the uniting King. For all honest Christians serve Jesus alone. Our traditions are secondary. In fact, they are worthless if we cease to have a heart for the King and fail to serve him alone. God wants his people to be at peace with each other. Therefore, let us tear down the fences! Let us truly serve the one and only God.

We are united under Jesus because he is so high above us. No person and no denomination may ever say, "Jesus is mine." You cannot create unity by expecting everyone else to have the same thoughts, or feelings, or beliefs as you. We will be united only when we all become subject to one Lord. This Lord belongs to everyone—all classes, all professions, all races. He is the "next of kin" to each individual. Once we accept him as the one Lord, who is high above us all, we will become one people. We are useless servants unless Jesus alone prevails.

# 6

## The Way of the Cross

WE MUST LEARN TO become silent before God and wait for him. To make a big noise in the name of God has never advanced anything. Those who make a big to-do not only ignore the cross but soon run out of steam. Everyone from Noah on has had to learn to become silent. Thousands of people have proclaimed, "I belong to the Lord," but the world has taken no notice. When the Savior said to his disciples, "Go into all the world" (Mark 16:15), his final words were, "I am with you always" (Matt 28:20)—which means, "Take heed, because it is not in your hands. I will do it."

Therefore, don't blow your own horn! If you want to start a sect or some new movement, then go ahead and make a lot of noise; if you want to be famous, then go ahead and sound off; but if you want to seek God's kingdom, then stand before the cross and be quiet. God's kingdom will not come into being by our efforts; only God can bring it about. We are not expecting an improved society. This is not what we are working for. God alone has the power to put the stamp of his divinity on human beings and to ennoble what is true and genuine in a human being.

In your personal life too, become quiet. Guard against exaggeration. And do not chatter so much about spiritual and religious matters. Don't think about yourself too much either. By becoming too preoccupied with ourselves, we end up talking too much and then take our salvation into our own hands. We need people who know they belong to God but who are quietly natural about it. We will never catch a glimpse of what God is doing by strenuous thinking—godly matters come unnoticed into our hearts. It is God who puts his truth into your heart through his Spirit, truth that will flow out of you by itself, like your breath.

⊷

The need of the world comes to the church of Jesus Christ. On the cross Jesus took our pain upon himself, and his example of bearing burdens applies to his church too. The suffering of this world comes, in some way or another, to those who want to follow Jesus. But they do not succumb to it, as others do, but silently endure it, overcoming the violent blows of sin. Because of this the world grows brighter and gets easier for people—easier for Jesus' followers, too.

That is why we should never say, "O God, spare me from this! I can't understand why I have to endure it. Haven't I always done what was right? Haven't I always prayed? And now this evil strikes me, just like it strikes the world!" No, we have to take upon ourselves the suffering of the world. After all, we can bear it, because Jesus is victor in us and through his suffering he conquers the evil that oppresses humankind.

We are called to help relieve the world. We must not separate ourselves from the world by not wanting to share in the world's life and suffering. Anyone who does this is like a branch broken off a tree. It stays green for a short time and then withers. We must remain connected to humanity's tree of life, no matter how cancerous the tree may be. In the end, all sorrow will cease, but in the meantime you will not be spared. You must carry the eternal within you, which will one day overcome the evil in this world.

But our task is to do more than carry the world's pain. We must be ready to be despised for Jesus' sake. We must pick up our cross and carry the Savior's pain—the burden that he carried when he hung on the cross, completely forsaken and misunderstood. That is actually the only real pain that we as his followers have. We have to shoulder his cross, and say, "Blessed are we when people ridicule and persecute us for Jesus' sake." It is high time that we take up this battle. All of us who are seeking the kingdom of God must be willing, and joyfully so, to be called "the forsaken ones." Nothing new ever comes without a fight, and in this fight we must be ready to die. But rest assured, whatever we suffer for the sake of Jesus will bear good fruit. The suffering of the cross always hastens the coming of God's kingdom. Woe to us if we hold it against people when they despise and persecute us! They can't help it. They don't know any better. We must forgive the world and patiently endure what it lays upon us.

⌖

Because Christ is with us, we dare not belittle a single person. We must be able to shed tears for sinners, but not get angry, hard, or judgmental toward them. If Christ is in us, we have no choice but to suffer alongside the multitudes and cry out, "Father, forgive them, for they do not know what they are doing."

Christ in the flesh has no teeth and no horns. He remains like a sheep before a shearer and leaves all things up to God. This is the yoke that the Savior calls "easy" (Matt 11:30). If we resist and despair over humanity and get angry about peoples' sins, then it will be terribly hard to follow Christ. Nothing is more depressing than being bitter about one's fate. However, if we readily follow the Lamb of God, who carried the sins of the world, it will be easy. It is easy because we are one with God and possess a clear conscience. It may be hard on our flesh, but to carry the cross, this cross of Jesus Christ, becomes easy with God.

⌖

To suffer rightly brings redemption. Granted, if we suffer on account of a misdeed, that has no value. But if we suffer innocently, then evil is overcome. Christ is our example. Suffer boldly, certain of victory, in the knowledge that Christ who is in you is stronger than your suffering. Hardship will pass away, but you will not. Be triumphant in the face of suffering.

⌖

Just as the Savior had his cross to carry, so must we. The fact that we have a cross is actually proof that we are near him. Because Jesus had compassion toward the world's guilt, the world became his cross. When Jesus calls someone to be his disciple, he is calling you to join the company of sufferers. First he sets you free by saying, "You are a child of God. Your sins are forgiven." But then he adds, "Whoever does not carry their cross cannot be my disciple" (Luke 14:27). So begins our participation in the need of the world. This participation goes deep and brings us into "collision" with the world. Our cross is to endure whatever the world throws at us. We would like to embrace the world with God's love, but it pushes us away—partly out of stupidity, partly through misunderstanding, partly due to despair.

In the beginning Pietism, for example, was a good and beautiful movement. It brought life into a rigid church—warm and heartfelt life that streamed from the Savior. Its members sought to embrace the world and did embrace it. Thanks to Pietism, many new works of love were done—works that had never been done before. But then the world struck back, maligning those who wanted renewal—and that became their cross.

When such a cross falls on you, be careful not to let yourself grow bitter. The Savior never responds to the world with bitterness. He sees the ignorance of people and forgives them. The cross of Jesus bears good fruit because it remains in God's love. And wherever there exists something of God's love, Christ's redemptive work is present. A cross in and of itself is not worth anything—God's love has to accompany it. This love is beyond our human power or comprehension. Whoever wants to take up his cross better realize that love must be present. If you will not love, then stay away from Christ's cross. If you have been insulted and can't forget it, then stay away from Christ. We have to be people in whom God's *whole love* radiates. That love is the strongest power in the world. Jesus is victor over sin and evil because of God's great love. Without this love, faith and zeal don't achieve much in God's kingdom. It is love alone that judges perfectly, builds soundly, and redeems. Suffering love reconciles heaven and earth and brings us back to God.

Christ did not suffer heroically. Rather, he came to dissipate the world's sorrows by taking them on himself. Christ "himself bore our sins in his body on the cross" (1 Pet 2:24). He did not shake off our sins but in love held on to them firmly. In so doing he united himself deeply with sinners. He submitted himself so that he could unite with everyone and bring them to the place where the fire of God's love separates the sinner from the sin.

This is how it should be for his church on earth. The Lord in heaven and his church on earth continue to carry the world's injustice and thereby dissipate it. Even sins, when they are carried in Christ, can be dissolved. It is never in vain to grapple with sin in our longing for God. Sin must cease in you and be transformed into righteousness. Death must cease and become life. But how are sin and death to be overcome if Christ has no followers on earth? If no one on earth offers themselves up, then there will continue to be tears in heaven. No matter what you have to suffer—even the smallest evil—carry it, looking up to God for the sake of the world. Give it over to Jesus, so that it can be dispelled.

⟿

If you tell people to their face about their sins they will not respond. Their ears and their hearts are already blocked by sin. You will not be able to speak to people's hearts by taking a frontal attack. Part of their inner being may respond, but their deepest being will flee away. No. There is only one way to preach to people—the way the Savior showed us. He was like a lamb before the shearer. He bore our sins. And today he carries them with his blood and by his death. As followers of Jesus Christ we, too, must carry sin. We have to bear the sins of the world before God without sparing ourselves. In other words, we must be silent and suffer like Christ—we must carry in our hearts the sin of this world before God and say unflinchingly, "What is being done is not right. It is a sin." Then wherever we go and whomever we meet there will be in us a living witness against sin. We will not have to use many words. People will feel it. Please don't spout off to people in their face about their sin. That won't be of any use. Giving them a sermon never helps. We must preach by our inner attitude. Our calling is not to judge people. We have been given the task of preaching the way Jesus did on the cross—by quietly suffering.

People have to realize for themselves their own sin. This comes through *God's* judgment, not ours. Only then will they come to God. When we suffer among the people for God's sake, we can do no more than bring it to God and sigh, "When will this people open their eyes?" This attitude is the kind of sermon people need. When a pastor preaches in this inward way, when he looks for God's truth and lives by it, when he cries out for mercy and grace and judgment, so that sins are revealed through the Spirit, then things start to happen. The whole world is affected, even though he may never leave the confines of his own church.

It is this kind of preaching that anticipates the last judgment, when "All peoples on earth will mourn" (Rev 1:7). You and I can never make people mourn. No one can. But what we preach in our spirit before God penetrates into their unconscious, into the invisible domains where everything comes out, both the good and the bad. We must preach into this domain; we must draw God into this realm; we must declare there, "We will not tolerate it anymore. In the name of Jesus, we will no longer tolerate those hidden streams of sin that keep people in bondage."

We must never condemn the sinner, ever! We must condemn the sin and the temptation that leads to sin, but not people. Our task is to get out from under the spell in which all of us live. We ourselves must be changed people. We have to keep ourselves right and true. For if we allow the unclean streams of this world into our lives, how can we ever work on God's behalf? How can we ever proclaim to the nations their transgressions? And this proclamation is pure love and pure good news.

Jesus does not repay evil with evil—he remains with his Father in heaven. In heaven there are no fist fights or duels; there is no slandering or despising. In heaven love is practiced on a large scale. Even criticism submits to love; admonition is no longer something devastating but freeing and redeeming. What Jesus says never hinders or harms. He can even say, "You hypocrites!" or "You belong to your father, the devil" (John 8:44), because these very words lead to salvation. They are spoken on God's turf, and God despises no one.

A gardener sometimes has to tie a plant up. When necessary, he also prunes—even to the roots. But whatever he does, he tries to rescue his plants. Similarly, "God so loved the world that he gave his one and only son" (John 3:16), so that everything might be rescued. This is why Jesus associated with tax collectors and sinners. He kept company with the despised precisely because, even though they still had evil within them, they were ready to open themselves to him. He knew he could use them. He connected with their faith and waited patiently until the evil in them left.

This is the Jesus we follow. When everyone else scolds, we shall not. When everyone else condemns, we will refuse. When everyone else turns their backs, we will look and see if we can find the one involved who may need our help most. Let it never be said of us, "They repay evil with evil." No! We are those who forgive sins wherever we go.

Have you ever noticed what great warmth comes into your heart whenever you forgive sins? There is nothing greater, nothing more blessed, nothing that lifts our spirits more than this power to forgive sins. Certainly without Christ himself who stands behind us, we would not have the courage to meet people (who are often full of darkness) with the authority to forgive sins. But if Jesus stands behind us, we have that authority. Anyone can judge and condemn—the world does plenty of that! The authority given to us is the strength to forgive without judging and condemning.

In this forgiveness of sins resides the power of God's Spirit to create new people. When we say, "You belong to God," we are saying that everything about a person can change. Even if the impulse to sin is still in you and you find yourself falling back into sin, your life can still come under the power of God's forgiveness. Therefore, be comforted—your true self will come out all right. Your true self belongs to God. And once you realize this, you will want to give up your selfishness. Open your hands. Let everything go. The main thing is that your own inner being grows and emerges into your true self, who comes from God. God's Spirit will see to it that you find perfection.

⋄

We have to learn anew what it means to take guilt upon ourselves. So many people say, "I'm not to blame. I haven't sinned." No one wants to admit they have sinned or done something wrong, even when they find themselves despairing in all their need. All the more we Christians should learn to pray the way Daniel prayed (Daniel 9). He included himself among the guilty and even took on himself the guilt of his fathers, whose sins were responsible for the great disaster. He was filled with remorse, "We have received our just deserts, and if it weren't for God's great mercy, there would be no help for us, because God is righteous." Daniel's prayer was heard—and if we would but pray like Daniel, our prayers would be heard, too.

Instead of praying like Daniel, however, we grumble, especially when things don't go well or our way. We can't bring ourselves to admit, "I deserve it." So our prayers are fruitless, worthless. In fact, God is offended when someone grumbles. Just those who are best are the ones who must humble themselves the most and repent. They must see the sorrow and misery of the past, and because the sins of their fathers have been passed down to them, they must humble themselves beneath their load. If we want to achieve anything, then any other attitude is a mistake. Only in humility can we be fruitful and find the heavenly blessings that are promised us.

⊹

Every truth is hated when it is first introduced. It's not that people don't *want* to know the truth, they simply can't. They are scared of it. Again and again this fear of the truth threatens to destroy the very One who, full of grace and truth, came into the world. This devil of human fear, which so easily turns into hatred, is what crucified and keeps crucifying Jesus. And so the devil continues to persecute, hate, and slander those who represent truth in the world. So shall it be, and so shall it continue until darkness is once and for all removed from this world.

⊹

If you are a disciple of Jesus, rest assured, no one will flatter you. Try as you like, the world will hate you. God's presence in you will never be understood until the day Jesus Christ comes. The world never understood the Savior, so witnesses who have God's presence in them today will not be understood either. The more God's power flows from you, the more you will be rejected. You will not be understood even though you sacrifice your body and soul for people. Every disciple of Jesus must count on being hated. We have to live through it and not worry too much about it. Have no fear of the world, the worst it can do is kill us!

⊹

True fighters for Jesus are not offended when people hate them. Whoever feels insulted, whoever strikes back when he receives a blow for the sake of truth, is not a true fighter for Christ. The whole struggle for God's kingdom consists in laying down your life for others. In this way, even the people who hate us shall receive life. The light of Christ's life enables me to be faithful unto death—I would rather die than let my love to the world be stolen from me.

We will always make mistakes, like arguing too much with other people. But let our aim be to give witness to life only in friendship and goodness, for God is faithful to all people. Like our crucified Lord, let us bear silently any opposition we face, even from our worst enemy, firmly holding on to the truth that all people belong to God. Let us fight that more and more people realize this. Let us hold on to the faith that God will help each sinner turn into a good person. People will not slander and hate forever. The more faithful we are, the more hate against us will be burned away. Hate has a short life. It is love that lives forever.

⊕

Our notion of human "rights" stands in opposition to God's justice. We think we possess all sorts of rights: fathers think they have rights to their children; men feel they can assert their rights over women; and on it goes. All of us tend to make a right out of anything, especially when it concerns us and our station in life. In so doing, we end up using our "rights" to oppress or control other people. That is why Jesus says, "All who have come before me are thieves and robbers" (John 10:8).

But I ask: When do you see Jesus ever demanding his rights? He "did not consider equality with God something to be used to his own advantage" (Phil 2:6). He did not make it a right that he was born to be above all other human beings. Instead, he emptied himself and became the servant of all. He renounced his rights. Jesus said, "Whoever wants to be my disciple must deny themselves" (Matt 16:24)—must renounce their rights. In other words, when we *demand* our rights we are inhuman. Only when we *renounce* our rights do we become truly human.

Where then are the followers of Jesus who are willing to forgo their rights, to go the lowly way, in order to become true human beings? Where are the people who are ready to sacrifice their rights and appeal to God and to God's justice alone? Only when we represent God's justice on earth as God's servants can we help people. Only then is God honored as the protector of justice for all people.

⊕

The highest goal of fellowship with God is the maturing and perfecting of our true self, our worth as an individual. This is why our relationship with God can never be defined or governed by laws. The law does not regard individual differences. This doesn't mean we are free to ignore the law in our relationships with other people. Freedom from the law in my relationship with God is what enables me to endure human laws that govern my relationships with others. Freedom toward God helps me, so to speak, to be a servant here on earth. I am still free, but in my freedom before God I overcome evil with good.

This is why Christians must not use their freedom for revolutionary purposes. We cannot bring about goodness in the world with a strong arm, or with a sword, not by fist against fist. Our freedom in Christ enables us inwardly, not politically, to overcome the bondages of this world. With our freedom we are called to work our way into the world's slavery so that God's will is revealed. In our freedom we deliver up the worldly spirit for dissipation, but we are not the ones who dissipate it. We give what is human over to death so that what is divine may live in what is human.

‹›

Give each person time and space. Only then will they be able to serve God and further love in their own way.

‹›

We should not destroy old ways before we have found new ways.

‹›

For God to rule, he needs free people, not revolutionaries. We can be free without overthrowing anything. We can be free in all circumstances, free under God's rulership, in the certainty that God, the Father, and Jesus, the King, will change whatever needs to be changed. The world is under God's control—we are not commissioned to rule the world.

Those who are free in God are remarkably strong, even though they may be under someone else's authority. They experience genuine progress, just because they are free and do not get involved in money-making deals. They leave everything in God's hands. They only take action when something falls into their laps. What makes us weak and unfree is when we think that we can't be true Christians unless we first change our circumstances. But the cross shows us that we do not need to change anything! This is the great cancer that has crept into Christian circles over the centuries: that people think they have to do things for which they are not created. We are created to be children. As children we may be like this today and like that tomorrow. Sometimes our Father marches forth, then we march forth with him. Sometimes our Father is silent, then we also are silent. Sometimes our Father uses a loud voice, then we do, too. Sometimes our Father scatters us, and then we separate. When he beckons to us again, we come together. Only in our submission to God are we truly faithful. Then we think of nothing except, "My Lord and my God, you do everything!"

❦

As disciples of Jesus, we are like sheep among wolves. That is just about the opposite of what we see in history, where people usually fight, tooth and nail, for their existence. "Survival of the fittest" means that the weak perish—but Jesus opposes this. No! The strong shall perish and the weak shall live. There is no future on earth for anything coarse, rude, sarcastic, cutting, or killing. So give up the fight for existence. Jesus gave it up on the cross. He surrendered his cause to the Father in heaven and died. Make peace with everyone and rely on God's Spirit. Be like sheep among wolves.

In any way possible, tear out your fangs. Don't bite anymore! Don't shove! Don't punch! Don't pick a fight unnecessarily! Even if you think you are right, you do not have to snap at people like a wolf or a tiger. Be more like a lamb, and when the wolf begins to growl angrily, just leave. You don't have to kill the wolf, just turn away and let him howl. But if you have to leave, then go joyfully in God's love: "Jesus lives! This is my life." If you do this, your enemies will get the message. But remember, when you testify do it in God's love, tenderly with respect. We must be noble and sensitive, so that people can see by our behavior what great love God has for them.

❦

If we want to win the world for God's cause, we must go about it quietly. We have to be like a hunter when he goes into the woods. He walks about very quietly, otherwise all the game runs away.

❦

Jesus is God's suffering servant. In him goodness, truth, and justice are personified. It is good when someone does not break a bruised reed (Isa 42:3), when they do not completely trash or condemn poor, bruised people, or try to force them to change. Instead, with the light given to them from God, they should help whatever goodness is left in the bruised and corrupted person to blossom again.

Jesus quietly draws the almighty God down to earth, so that darkness is driven away and goodness comes forth. He never chased after the Pharisees. No, it was they who came to him. Jesus keeps himself free, and anyone who wants to be with Christ must do the same. He must deny himself, and in quiet gather with others around Jesus, letting his light come naturally to others. Then the various bondages that people are under, the inhibitions of their lives and the cords of death that threaten to strangle them, will break, and they will become new people.

⊕

I urge you not to complain so much about the things you find difficult in life. When you talk a lot about all that makes life difficult, you only make things worse. The person who looks for a friend so that they can "off load" their grievances ends up gossiping their way into hell. Become quiet and look up to the Father in heaven, to whom you belong. When you do this, a door into heaven opens.

⊕

I have made this a practice: if something doesn't easily come about, I don't pray for it to happen anymore. In my experience, when I undertake some action and God is with me, then a little prayer is enough. But when things become too difficult, or when I feel myself having to strive, then I need to become quiet and think, "God doesn't want to do it for me quite yet." I am very careful not to say, "I will do it anyway, so help me God!" Any zeal on my part, or any forcing—"I am going to do it anyway"—is wrong. We must wait for the time when God will do it.

⊕

Jesus is not ashamed to call us brothers. So what about us? Those who are educated are often ashamed to be with those who are not; "good" people don't like to mix with those who are shady. But a truly holy person, a saint, never separates himself from the profane—he overcomes godlessness. The Savior calls us brothers and sisters—yet we condemn people right and left, throwing them straight into hell. We have become incapable of standing with each other as brothers and sisters. Rays of sunshine are needed to change people. But they can only do so if they touch them. Likewise, God's power comes close to people, bringing the divine qualities in them to the surface. God's power will convert the world.

⊕

When the Savior brought God's love into the world, he remained holy. He did not sully himself with worldliness. He went to the tax collectors and the sinners, but he didn't become a tax collector or a sinner. When he associated with prostitutes and adulteresses, he was not guilty of any offense. The opposite happened: God's love judged and then freed people. Jesus came to sinners, and they were struck in their consciences and felt the need to change.

⊕

We have to understand love in a new way. But don't think too much about it—just be like children and accept it. Let the love with which God loved the world come into your hearts through the Holy Spirit. The Spirit of God radiates love—there is no condemnation in him. God's Spirit is love. He is the same Spirit who spoke into the darkness, "Let there be light!" When God's love speaks, the world is made new. In Jesus Christ it will again be made new. God's love will penetrate everything, and the hate that has made its dwelling in us will be destroyed. Believe in Jesus Christ and hate will be no more. To believe in Jesus, means to love. Receive God's love into your hearts, and then you will be freed from sin. You *will* become a new creation.

⊕

God's love makes us free. Whoever loves his fellow human beings is free—whoever hates them is a slave. Whoever lives in peace with other people is free—whoever lives in a state of war is a slave.

⊕

To be a servant of God, your spirit must be noble and unfettered. You will need to have a very large vision of God's kingdom, one in which everyone and everything belongs to it. Division and disunity have harmed God's cause again and again. If you want to serve Jesus, who is King of kings and Lord of lords, you must understand that the world belongs to God, and that God does not want to relinquish any part of it. You must see that Christ lays claim on everyone—whether high or low, good or bad. Everything that lives belongs to God. And this truth should be not only in our heads but in our blood, in every breath. As a servant of Jesus Christ, do not give up on anyone—even the worst sinner. We have to believe for ourselves and for others that we all belong to God. I may be stupid and clumsy—I may even commit sin—but my true self, which is created in God's image, belongs to God. Neither sin nor death can change this fact.

Give me the sinners! Give me the perverted! Don't throw them out of my house! Don't tear them out of my heart! Let me try to live in brotherhood with the lost, with all those who are considered sinners. Give me the freedom to search among people who are in bondage. I do not want to go to the righteous who have fled to the desert.

Do not give up on yourself—never! You must believe in yourself for God's sake. That is not egoism—it is valuing what God has created in you. I am not permitted to trash anyone, least of all myself. No person is evil at the core. They are merely entangled in evil. As soon as I have recognized that I am unworthy, then the nobler part of myself that God originally created will be born in me.

A truly evil person doesn't recognize their wickedness. Consider the centurion from Capernaum who said to Jesus, "I do not deserve to have you come under my roof" (Matt 8:8). But then he added, "But just say the word"—send your word under my roof. Similarly, when you know that in spite of sin and guilt you belong to God, you will feel called to live for others—yes, the whole world can be laid on your heart. Like the centurion, who asked on behalf of the servant who lived under his roof, so the whole world can be under your roof and you can pray for it. Abraham thought of all generations on earth (Gen 22:18). Hannah and Mary in their songs of praise carried all nations on their hearts (1 Sam 2:1–10; Luke 1:46–55). A child of God is called to be concerned for the whole world. We should not tolerate the hells that people live in. God has made all of us to be kings and priests.

✧

God's chosen ones cannot make Christ King themselves. God must administer justice to them for their King. It lies in God's power alone to glorify his Son Jesus Christ, so that he is recognized on earth for who he truly is. That is why his chosen ones must pray. We are called to pray. Our happiness is to see Jesus honored and to be able to say, "We helped him. We looked to God alone and prayed to God that he would crown this King."

✧

If we are messengers for God, then we can proclaim salvation, preach peace, and speak about goodness to all people—the great and the humble, the rich and the poor, the just and the depraved. We do not talk about misery, perversity, or godlessness anymore. The whole world laments about that already; so does every individual who weeps over their own imperfection and sin, over the impossibility of ever doing any real good. In the name of the Father, you must remember that the crucified Jesus strides into this misery, under which people suffer terribly, and proclaims the good news: "Your sins have been forgiven. Be comforted. The godlessness, the wickedness that is all around you, and that has also taken root in you and embittered your life, will not be triumphant. It will be wiped out—forgiven. You belong to God, to your Father in heaven. You will become good; you will become just; you *will* find salvation. No matter what sin oppresses you, and no matter what sickness or affliction torments you, it will all be taken away. Salvation is coming!"

So now let us preach the triumph of goodness and proclaim salvation. And when we do, believe that people can once again do what is good. People need to sense that we trust them, that they are God's children, and that deep down they have a feeling for what is right. Trust the people, preach the good news, then you will find the way to their hearts. Wherever you go, believe that people can become good, in the name of the Savior.

The Apostle Paul writes, "Do everything in love" (1 Cor 16:14). It is not easy, however, to do *everything* in love. To hold firmly to love in everything, in all the silly, little things of daily life—that is a hard job. It is in the small things that we so easily misunderstand people and fail to love them. It is as though the daily affairs of life have a power to constantly irritate us. We get upset by constant gibes, biting comments, quick-tempered actions, and general unpleasantness.

But Paul writes, "Do everything in love." This means that it is stupid not to love in daily things, foolish to lose the great and noble love that come to us through Jesus who died for us. We are called to remain above these mundane and small things, responding only with love. Love should guide our understanding more than anything else. But love is not a warm feeling. Nor does it have anything to do with flattery, which disappears like snow in the sun and breaks down with the first small incident. Real love remains above in the strength of God and the Spirit of Jesus Christ. If we don't embrace this understanding of love, we will not be victorious in daily life.

If you rely on the Father's love, you will find yourself, so to speak, on a mountain. The higher up you go, the greater will be the horizon of your love. As you go up the mountain of the Lord, you will be astonished—the higher you go, the further your love will reach. Continue going up until you can love all people, like God loves the world. On the mountain of God's love, you will be allowed to become more like him. You will learn to understand the thoughts of God that cover the whole creation. But it takes patience and faith to climb to the top of this mountain. Even so, how much is accomplished if even only a few people climb to the top. Oh, how the light will shine! Therefore, place yourself on the Father's mountain and become holy like God is holy. Love the way God loves. He will give you a tremendously great view—the kingly attitude of Jesus Christ.

Jesus, the crucified Savior, is the only one who has ever loved all people without exception. We, on the other hand, have the audacity to think that we will be saved while others will not. Jesus doesn't acknowledge any such boundaries. He loves us in advance, before we are "worthy" of his love. He loves us before God's kingdom has fully come. He loves us while we are sinners, because his love comes from eternity. But just because of that, judgment is combined with his love. His love is not soft. It does not overlook our sin. That is not love. Jesus' love hangs on the cross and works in us so that we are purified. Jesus' love is our salvation. This is the gospel, "You are loved."

Therefore, we must love each person with Christ's love. And that is not easy. All too often we meet people who look dark and repulsive. They don't want to be loved; they want to look after themselves. All the more we have to love them in the Spirit of Jesus, not with things of the earth, but in the Spirit. Let no partition separate "them" from "us" anymore. There is hope for all. Love those who are repulsive or dark. Love your enemies. Bestow your love on miserable places, even in hell. Hate the evil, but not the people who do evil; with the Savior, look past the ugly exterior of people's lives and into their hearts. Have you ever looked into someone's *heart* and found it to be unworthy of love?

I believe firmly in Christ's love. There is a tremendous power in it. It can convert people and conquer whole nations and whole societies without them even noticing it.

Who knows, perhaps God's kingdom has been delayed just because we again and again set limits, because we have not sufficiently understood our vocation as followers of Christ, which is to regard *everyone* as a future citizen of God's kingdom. Do you think that people will be converted outside of the cross? No! Never! We must bring them into God's kingdom by loving them as Jesus does. Only then will the chains fall that still bind them. God's kingdom will envelop all people before they know it, and this will slowly start to change their lives. They will be given different hearts and new thoughts. Then the time will come when their deepest needs will be met.

Let us unite with the Savior of the world and believe that something of the kingdom has already begun. His kingdom has no limits because it is *God's* kingdom.

⌀

In the Sermon on the Mount the Savior says, "You have heard that it was said, 'Love your neighbor and hate your enemy'" (Matt 5:43). Notice, he did not say, "*God* said to the people long ago." It had just come down to the people long ago, but God did not say it. Then the Savior says, "But I tell you"—I tell you what God alone says and has always said, "Love your enemies and pray for those who persecute you, that you may be children of your Father in heaven . . . Be perfect, therefore, as your heavenly Father is perfect" (Matt 5:44–48). If you want to be perfect as your Father in heaven is perfect, then regard people as people and lay aside their incompetence, which is none of your business anyway.

God doesn't treat sinners differently from the righteous. He died for all people! If a sinner fares worse than a righteous person, it is his own fault. If someone runs away from God's goodness and God's protection, then that person will have to suffer a life that is not under God's protection. Even so, the sun will still shine on them. No one can remove themselves completely from God's love. But don't think that God's love is soft or makes one soft. The opposite is true—it makes one noble. God's love is holy, and like the sun, it is high above the sphere of human love. The sun rejects no one. Neither does God. Although God rejects sin and allows us to suffer the consequences of sin, he never rejects people.

Like the sun, we must also shine God's love on people. Because of the Savior, the nail of sin has been loosened. When a nail in a board becomes loose, you can pull it out. But if I judge and condemn sinners, I am hammering the nail of sin back in and even bending it over so it can't come out. Our task is to love, to demonstrate God's great mercy—to pull the nail of sin out. God in his love wants to separate the sin from the sinner.

In Israel God's face was portrayed—to be sure it was a changing face: sometimes angry (as in Elijah) or serious (as in Jeremiah). The whole history of Israel shows God's features. If you read the pages of the Old Testament you will surely see the facial features of God. You will see him, so to speak, as a man. People of old looked at what was around them—they didn't look for God in the distance, but close at hand. This is what gave Israel its strong and distinctive character.

The cross of Jesus Christ also shows the face of God. But this face cannot be portrayed in wood or stone. God's image is shown in his Son, in the Word being made flesh, and continues to shine in the lives of men and women who let him rule in their hearts. God blesses creation through people, and thus we see his countenance in those who give themselves to God.

Even whole villages can present a picture of God's face. I remember once as a child in Möttlingen, when the Holy Spirit was at work in many hearts, when strangers would come and visit and say, "We feel like we are coming into a living room in God's house. We can enter any cottage and be welcomed." God wants us to reflect his image so that people can say, as it were, that his face is mirrored in our faces. This is the task of the church: to let the countenance of God shine in the world—the love and goodness and goodwill of God, in all truth and justice, in all seriousness and friendship. The church should portray the real picture of who God is in such a way that all other images are forgotten and done away with.

⊸

The first apostles thought they would experience Christ's return in their lifetime. But they had to learn to be patient. They came to realize that there were still many unconquered "elements" (2 Pet 3:10, 12) or as the Apostle Paul expresses it, "rulers, authorities, . . . and the spiritual forces of evil in the heavenly realms" (Eph 6:12). These powers make up the foundation on which this world is built. They have yet to be overcome. Unwillingness and hate, and above all thoughtlessness and apathy have taken hold of people, and in this state the pleasures of the world continue to oppose God. Hence, there is hardly a one who is free for the gospel.

That is why only a few people believe the gospel of a "new creation" as Paul calls it. These few must wait for the Lord's return. But in their waiting they must fight with burning hearts. The new life promised in the gospel is like a fire. It burns up what is false in us, and then sets on fire the elements of this ungodly world with holy flames. But first, we ourselves have to be burned up. Inside us, "The heavens will disappear with a roar; the elements will be destroyed by fire" (2 Pet 3:10). Then the powers of darkness will no longer be able to rule in us. We have to ask God, "Do not spare us. Let your fire burn, and show us how nothing false can exist wherever Jesus rules."

Out of compassion for humanity we should be asking for this fire, because our preaching isn't going to get us any further. Everything stays the same if all people hear are words. We have to become so full of fire, so closely connected to the powers of heaven, that it becomes obvious that the powers of darkness have been lifted from us, and that whatever lives in the darkness gets revealed and burned in the fire until it is purified.

Jesus Christ needs a church that is on fire. If we don't burn for him and for his coming Day, he will not have the means to set the world on fire. This is what is missing—no one is on fire! Sure, people campaign for this or that or espouse this or that brand of Christianity, they dispute about doctrine and approaches—but all this is a score for Satan, who loves to sow dissension in the church. So let us give up all our religious strife and opportunism. We are expecting a new heaven and a new earth. On the cross, Christ defeated the principalities and powers. Therefore, turn your back on human ways and means, and be a blazing fire for God so that a firebrand can be lit at your fire and be thrown into the world.

We can all be firebrands. But we have to remain high above what is humanly possible and let go of what is humanly fashionable. We have to rise to a higher level, like Jesus, who was in the world but not of it. We must cut the tiny thread that keeps pulling us down to the world and its fleeting desires. We must arise high enough to let the things of this world burn up beneath us.

Our own gifts and capabilities never accomplish anything. Whenever we rely on them the light inside us goes out. No. We can stand above the elements of this world and also endure the troubles of our time with the same patience with which Jesus endured his suffering. His patience was a power that led to resurrection, and it remains in us a power for resurrection. But it takes a fight before people are completely free. However, bit by bit, and person by person, a fire can be lit and then spread. The fire of Christ burns and will set aflame all those ready to be burned. From them it will spread right into the Day of Jesus Christ.

# 7

# Hope and Expectation

WE OFTEN SPEAK OF a lost Paradise. No, our paradise is in the future.

The kind of death we are to fight is not temporal death, not transference into the hereafter, which can even be a joy in certain cases. Death itself is not what causes distress in our life. Actually it is in the pangs of death that something higher is born in us. No one can amount to anything if they are weak and spineless. We should not wish the crises of life to be removed.

Real death comes to us when we do not know how to continue in our responsibilities, when we are cast down in spirit. Death presses down on us as long we are caught up in the march of time and in the wheels of the world, when we cannot see more than the past, or beyond money, house, and land. This is death. Death gets a hold of a nation if it cannot break away from its nationalistic concepts.

We must be on guard against this kind of death. The church of Jesus Christ, in particular, has to be free, as free as a bird. It must show by example how to live—not make cozy nests for itself and fight for them as if they were more vital than God. Only when the church of Jesus Christ remains inwardly free can it bring life to this world of death.

Why does the Savior fight so much against sickness and death? In certain cases, isn't it happiness to die? Doesn't everything in this world eventually come to an end anyway? As with every plant and animal, each one of us will reach an end when our life will cease. All this is true. But when Jesus fights death, he is not simply in opposition to the cessation of life. If he was, he would be opposed to the harvest. An apple ripens, and then falls from the tree; wheat ripens, and then has another service to perform. Similarly, when an individual's life comes to fruition, he then has a service to perform elsewhere. Since the most important thing in him is the spirit, fruition may even come early. Some people are ready for death when they are still children. In this sense, they have matured, and having completed their task they die and serve elsewhere. A person's age is not the decisive factor. This is why life's most important question is, "Have you completed your mission on earth?" If you have, you can die joyfully. Jesus said, "It is finished." Not being finished, well, *that* is death.

Jesus also said, "Whoever believes in me will not die, even though he meets death. I will make him whole. I will cancel his shortcomings. I am the resurrection and the life. What I began on earth I will complete for the crippled and the lame, the blind and the deaf. For anyone who believes in me and lives in me, there is life—growth into eternity. Your hour has come, death is no more!"

Sorrow lies in our failure to fulfill our mission, to become whole. We weep in the face of death because we drag along so much that is unfinished. But God wants to wipe away these tears from our eyes. He will forgive our failings, he will make right whatever is broken and set us on a new footing. What we have not been able to finish, he will accomplish for us, if this is our deepest longing. This is the promise of the resurrection. What Adam and Eve did not accomplish in Paradise will be finished and what we have failed to do will be completed. There is always hope.

People today are caught up in achieving this or that. But they will never achieve anything unless death is overcome. Death is stagnation. Without the resurrection there is no growth, either for individual families, or generations, or nations, but only stagnation and decline. Everything comes to a standstill, people become desperate, and then life goes crazy, as it were.

Therefore let us wish for the growth that leads to fruition. Let us pray for growth in the Spirit—the Spirit who created the world, who forms the crystals and rocks, produces the plants, creates the animals, and who works most of all in people. This Spirit has such compelling power that it can heal our bodies and help us grow toward perfection. Let us live and believe in the One who is the resurrection and the life. He will not let us come to a standstill.

⊶

People who depend on God work quietly. They "wait patiently" (Rom 8:25). This patience, however, gives rise to an energy that is directed toward what they desire to achieve. It looks forward to the healing of human nature itself, to "the redemption of our bodies."

Natural science maintains that a living creature develops according to its aims. Insects protect themselves from being eaten by birds by assuming the color of a leaf or a twig, so that the birds are fooled. In northern countries the fur of the hare turns white like the snow. Here, a hare can hardly be distinguished from a clod of earth. Animals adapt themselves in accordance with the purpose of their lives. But we human beings fail to live according to the purpose of our life. When we look at a hare, we must bow our heads in shame and admit, "You are as you should be. I am not." It is this discrepancy between our ideals and our lives that causes us much grief. Who we ought to be is at variance with the way we are. We often don't think, but just follow our feelings. In fact, we control neither our thoughts nor our behavior. No wonder we often pursue aims in life that demand more than our physical strength allows. Or we have physical strength but with no vision how to use it. We are imperfect—at odds with ourselves. Our natures bring us to a deadlock. This is death.

But through the resurrection of Jesus Christ there is hope. Christ's resurrection amazes us, but it is remarkable only because we mainly see it at the final stage. If we would see its beginning we would understand it better. Right from his birth everything in Jesus was directed toward his resurrection. God's purpose for him (to be a genuine human being) was why a real human birth took place. His glorious humanity touched people, making right what was wrong and healing what was broken.

Jesus is the Son of Man, and as the Son of Man we must not overemphasize his divinity. Instead, we must grow in the knowledge of his humanity, which assures us that our whole life can be transformed. Jesus is the true man. Our fellowship with him enables us to grow into true human beings (so that even our physical life can develop according to God's purpose), and this, in turn, can give birth to a human society that is worthy of existence—that is a church of Jesus Christ, a body of Jesus Christ. How precious it is to be able to find resurrection and live, even in our bodies, in accordance with God's purpose!

If you want to be a disciple of Jesus, then really follow him, be happy in hope and persevere in patience. Don't waste your energy on religious and Christian disputes, but direct your heart toward becoming truly human. May God rouse people once more to expect "the redemption of the body."

God promises us that he will transfigure our lowly bodies, our very selves, too, and enable us to enter the heavenly kingdom in such a way that no bodily temptation can cause us to fall. But we do not have to only wait— some of this can happen now. Jesus Christ can already begin to transform us. Everything God accomplishes in us sprouts from a simple, natural seed. Even today the whole of our being can come into God's hands. Let us accept God's will, not only in the little attic room of our spirit, but deep down in our flesh. Let us resolve to keep his name holy in all that we do. It *is* possible. As people held by his hands, we can become completely free from all subjection to darkness.

When we speak of resurrection we have to imagine something quite simple. Trees, which were thought to be dead, may suddenly turn green again and blossom, becoming full of life. It will be similar with the resurrection. Although all our paths lead us downward toward death, one day our course will turn upward. This change will take place under the guidance of God, who works in quiet. The actual renewal of humankind will begin very quietly. "The Day of resurrection dawns in silence."

People think that when they die, everything will suddenly come right. But if we do not have eternal life here, what makes us think it will be better over there? Who gives us the right to think that when we die all the lies we believe in and all that is false in us will be removed? There are people who die and afterward are just as they were before—they see nothing and hear nothing but themselves. But for anyone who already possesses eternal life, God's life, laying aside the body has no great significance. A new and active life full of happiness begins.

⊕

Jesus Christ is the prince of life for us. However, this doesn't mean we automatically live the eternal life, nor does it mean we are living our lives to the full. Only a person who *lives* in eternity attains his full worth. Apart from eternity our lives suffer torment. But with Jesus and his everlasting life, we can be transferred into the eternal. All that torments us will be stripped off. In the eternal, all that is impure will be cleansed, all that is sinful and dying will be expelled. What is eternal belongs to God alone. But eternity is a reality, a world full of life. Neither Satan nor anything wicked or false can enter the eternal.

When our world comes into touch with the eternal, true life unfolds. Death is an interruption of life. Even if I don't come to an end, in death I can go no further. But if we live in the eternal now, there is ongoing life—we will grow and thrive ever higher toward God.

Jesus is the prince of life. But to a prince belongs a people, and these people have to be taught to live in the prince, as the prince lives in them. Jesus compares himself to bread, which he gives to his people to eat. He is the bread of life. He wants to be the eternal in us, so that we will also become eternal in him. He who brings eternal life never ceases to exist—he outlasts all eras and generations. Therefore, every person can hope to meet this prince of life.

⊕

The ancient Jews believed that the fulfillment of people's deepest need was approaching but not yet here. Because of this, there is embedded in Jewish history a desire to go forward, an urge for development. The Jews lived in the expectation of what had been promised to them. Even after receiving great revelations of God, they felt themselves poor. They did not look back and make gods out of their heroes. Greater things lay ahead of them, not behind them.

And this promise of greater things always remains on a realistic, human plane—without fanaticism. According to God's promise all creation will someday live harmoniously together, but not before us human beings have changed. None of the prophets ever proposed the founding of an ideal state, a society based on good laws and institutions with people left as they are. No, they knew of something much better: the kingdom of heaven that is to come to a people whose hearts have been changed. This great urge to go forward, intrinsic in the people of Israel, had such a powerful effect that the appearance of Jesus Christ came in answer to it.

⊕

God wants a new heaven and a new earth. And in reality, humankind itself also wants something new. So God and the peoples of this earth are actually in agreement. Humankind wants to develop further, it wants to make progress. Strictly speaking, however, human beings have not really progressed. Old Assyrian business contracts show us people who were just like we are today, with the same feelings, the same desires. Humanity is still not released from its suffering. Nevertheless, we hope for improvement. In some way or another, we want to be perfected. And in this we are in agreement with God.

Therefore we should not despise anyone or any movement that strives for progress. In fact, the very idea of progress belongs to Christianity. Pagans remain in their old ways. In India, for example, the same castes have been in existence for thousands of years. But wherever there is even a small admixture of Christianity, things are thrown into a state of turmoil. Followers of Christ seek to live in harmony with the God who wants to make things new.

Unfortunately, the turmoil that exists among Christian people today is frequently caused by hatred. Christian revolutionaries, even if they think they are doing God a service, are not. God's way of progress is stimulated by love. The kind of change Jesus wishes to bring about is one in which the wretched, the oppressed, the sick, the despised are helped. Jesus is the representative of God's love, and he wants to pour this love out on all people. Despise no one, condemn no one, raise the lowly from the dust, treat each person as an equal—with love. Then everything will become new, heaven and earth, too. God loves the world, and so he wants to make all things new. Therefore, if you want progress love the world.

⊕

He who endures to the end will be saved (Matt 24:13). We must not stop until the end is reached. Then a fresh beginning can bring something quite new. Until then, difficulties will continue. Visible and invisible powers still have to be overcome, and their removal is like undergoing an operation. Toward the end of history we know there will be earthquakes and violent storms, pestilence and confusion, and wars among the nations. These disasters are not yet the end, but they will usher in the last days. And the end will come when all kinds of troubles, fraught with disaster and death, have served their purpose. Then salvation begins. Whoever calls upon the name of the Lord will be saved. That is the end; but, of course, at the same time it is the beginning of something new. For with God there is no ending without a new beginning. So sin will come to an end. Injustice, falsehood, abnormality, all that is not good will come to an end sooner or later. Then, God will start to freely reign.

You, Christian, should be determined to see to it that evil ends. For this to happen, you must not grumble about anything good. In the end, bad things perish, good things do not. And this is true for individual people; nothing that is good is destroyed, but everything that is not good perishes. Anyone unwilling to give up their sinful ways, who clutches their offenses and holds tight to them, stubbornly defying God, is in for big trouble. But not so for the person who lets go. That person has everything he needs. Those who stop clinging to the earth receive everything. God's kingdom, with all its glory, draws near to them.

Enduring to the end, however, does not mean standing in stubborn defiance in face of the world's evil. A person can also die of obstinacy, but that is a human ending, not a divine end. If people want to take away my house—all right, they can have it! If they want to take away my rights—all right, let them go ahead! Evil has an end, and so does the persecutor. Your soul, however, does not. So, let yourself be persecuted, let yourself be abused and cursed—it will soon stop. Pray for your persecutors. If you are good and hold to what is good, you have no reason to fear for yourself.

By yielding yourself entirely to God, you are praying for the end times. By letting go of evil, as well as the things of this world, you are helping to hasten on the end. Oh, if only we had more wisdom, if only we would let go and stop holding on to things that won't last. Endure to the end, and you will be saved.

⊕

The Savior's greatest longing is the fulfillment of God's plan: to establish his kingdom on earth, as it is in heaven. A heavy burden rests on anyone who feels deeply for the unspeakable suffering of the present-day world—his tender heart can hardly bear it. Therefore Jesus works with heart and soul to bring an end to this time of woe, and he gives us his commandments so that we can help, too. When he called his disciples, he did so with the view of bringing this age to an end, as quickly as possible. The Savior was urgently concerned to end this epoch. To put it in human terms, Jesus expected that he and his disciples would tear this world in two. But hardly anyone understood his eager expectation. Now we look wistfully back at this joyful, hopeful urgency. But we must do more than look back. We have to respond to this tremendous and urgent expectation by accepting Jesus' commandments and being filled full of compassion for all the unspeakable misery that is taking place now. Oh, that we may yearn more for the end to come at last!

When it says in the Bible, "The end of all things is near" (1 Pet 4:7), it does not mean that the end of God's working is near. It is only the things we have produced, in our independence from God, that are coming to an end. One day there will be an end to evil. Sin, death, and hell cannot be perpetuated. Good alone is everlasting. It is simply impossible for evil to endure forever. And because God exists, everything that exists apart from God will have to cease.

There is truth in what Nietzsche says—that God is dead. Of course he isn't really dead, but in the lives of people he is dead. They run after all kinds of things, listen to all sorts of things other than God, and when you speak to them about God, they are bored. It appears that our civilization simply doesn't need God anymore. Oh, there are plenty of gods that exist, but for the most part God himself is dead. When we get on the train and want to reach our destination we do not inquire whether the conductor is having a hard day, whether the stoker is suffering, whether the guard is afraid. We just want to get to our destination. And so we sit there, assuming we'll eventually get there. Likewise, science and technology do not need God. They are succeeding quite well without him. God is dead.

God, however, is not dead. God lives. He is the Alpha and the Omega, the beginning and the end, the living one. And everything in between is chaos, not just spiritual alienation in which people don't know where life is going, but real chaos. Certainly a beginning has been made, but we have not reached the end. Men and women are meant to share in working for the end, for God's kingdom on earth, but they don't. Already in Paradise, human beings were supposed to do their part—the serpent could not be defeated without human cooperation. But they did not do their duty: they let a breach come between themselves and God. And so the unfolding of life toward its end was stopped short.

In the chaos that was left behind, great prophetic personalities appeared, men who spoke forcefully, "The work must be finished! We have to surrender!" Then at last Jesus Christ came. He stands in the middle between the Alpha and the Omega. From the time the Christian church started, it should have lived constantly for the end, crying, "It will work out! It will be different! Our God lives! Our God is coming!" But it neglected its task. Whoever wants to work for God's final kingdom has to face trouble, fear, and death. The chaos in our world cannot be overcome without a fight. For the children of God, there is no comfortable state of blessedness on earth, but battle. We must always hold up the banner for God's rights unflinchingly in the face of everything that does not bow down to God.

If our hope is not fulfilled, what will become of our earth and of humankind? When the wolves of our civilization ravage the earth, what will happen? Today, nations are slaughtered by the thousands, and then people wonder why a good God allows such things to happen. Our little bit of Christianity won't save us from the terrible times when millions of people will be wiped out, unless God has people who share in the work for his kingdom. Only at the end, when God has his throne on earth and not just in heaven, will there be real progress. Not until then will the actual development of humankind go forward.

Let each one of us, therefore, be earnest with himself and get off his soft bed of Christian piety. Even if it costs you your life, go right in, into the thick of the fight. Do not shirk what is difficult or embarrassing. Stop only crying out to God for help in your miseries. No, be God's helper. Do something with your hope. Carry your cross and go into the hardest battle. Jesus is alive, he is victor, and he has given us our part to carry out.

⌁

Nothing can save this world before the end comes. So do not complain about the world. On its own it is helpless. For the time being, we can only be drops of dew in the world to make it sparkle a little. And we can preach this gospel to the world: Jesus is your Savior!

⌁

Never think that we will convert the whole world before the Day of Jesus Christ. We preach to the world because there are hungry souls everywhere, but we do not believe that the world will be conquered by our preaching. Our task is to help the world, to carry it on our hearts, and commend it to the love of God. Persevere in this love and be steadfast to the end.

⌁

The words, "Behold, I am coming soon," divide the history of the church into two epochs—a preliminary time and the actual time of God's kingdom.

God's kingdom began when the Savior came in the flesh. In this period we have the gospel, which is "God's power to save everyone who believes it." Here the kingdom of God is announced through the gospel, and it is established on earth by its heralds. But the rule of God in Christ does not yet prevail. It has only made a quiet beginning in the believers. For the rest of the world, the masses, even when they hear the gospel they remain under the grip of sin and death. Even though the light of hope shines into the world through the gospel—this light that makes God's love known to the world and prevents the darkness from being victorious—the people's lives are not yet free for God. They still lack power to conquer sin. God's new creation exists only in secret, only among the believers. These believers are the heralds of the kingdom of God. It is their calling to be true until death, fighting to claim the earth as God's possession until the Son of Man comes in the glory of his Father.

Not until then will the full power of God in Jesus Christ come to the nations, to the human masses. What Christianity and the gospel were unable to achieve before will then take place—namely, judgment. In gospel times, too, no one is justified and blessed without judgment. Yet in this last judgment many more things will be revealed. God will remove much of what we think is right and good—many things that God has only tolerated through the centuries. Until this judgment comes, the renewal of human-kind as a whole has to wait.

Therefore we should not lose heart if at present the world remains as it is and faith can maintain the struggle only in secret. This world is not lost forever on that account. It waits and yearns for the final revelation of God, when Christ will make his appearance as King of kings. Until then, every-thing depends on the faithfulness of the heralds. To them in particular, to the "chosen," to the "servants who wait for their Lord," comes the answer to their longing, "Behold, I am coming soon."

There is an "eternal gospel" promised in the Revelation of John (Rev 14:6). It comes after the fall of Babylon. "Babylon" represents all the efforts of human beings who, apart from God, try to help or save themselves. It is where people follow the urge to do everything to save themselves from the sinister, unhappy forces of destiny. Into this terrible human state and into this confusion comes the gospel.

First, there is the gospel as we have had it up until now, which has become marred. Its characteristic is to cause division. Individuals are torn away; churches are founded and then set apart from the pagans and from unbelieving nations. In the midst of this divided condition, we proclaim the name of Jesus Christ as the Lord of heaven and earth.

An erroneous idea, however, has found its way into this gospel—the fundamental error is that those who have separated themselves think they are better than the people they are separated from. But they are supposed to be separated for only one reason: to take God's love back into the world. They are meant to be a priestly people on behalf of others. In the Spirit, they should overcome the world. In the Spirit, they should get involved with the need of the world because they cannot be content to let it carry on without God. They should seek to bring the light of Christ into the world and work for the Day of Jesus Christ when the eternal gospel will come.

This eternal gospel causes no more splits. It does not separate people from each other. This gospel belongs to all people, to all pagans. It embraces heaven and earth and what is under the earth, the sea, and every abyss. Can't you already hear today the angel of the eternal gospel (Rev 14:6)? Human divisions will cease. Of course, some people will understand it, while others will be frightened by this gospel. But whether we understand it or not, the eternal gospel is coming. Even today people have stopped asking, "Are you a Christian?" and ask instead, "Do you fear God?" For the angel of the eternal gospel proclaims without discrimination: "Fear God, you nations, tribes, and tongues. Worship him who made heaven and earth. You are free. Babylon has fallen. You all belong to God!" (Rev 14:7–8).

The time is coming when God will not differentiate between those whom we consider to be the godly and the ungodly, the righteous and the unrighteous, the Christians and the pagans. Happy is he who is not offended by this Jesus, by this gospel.

It is not yet the time to see the Day of the Son of Man. Be patient. There is much work to be done before that day comes. We can easily set up false dates. But the Day of Jesus Christ will not be set by us—it comes from God. Readiness to wait and expectation for the Day of Jesus Christ is part of what it means to live for God's kingdom.

It has been necessary to preach the gospel to the nations in order to preserve the seed of truth. But now the seed-pod bursts open. Now is the time when Jesus will come. It is already coming. But we have to be ready for everything to change before he arrives. Do you think the Savior wants to reign in our world as it is now?

For the Savior it is the goal of God's kingdom that matters. But all our Christian striving for justice, truth, and life cannot reach this goal. We as individuals or congregations may wrestle and fight as much as we like, but the best we can do is to come under the great protection of God, so that the spirit of the world and the gates of hell cannot overpower us. But this is not yet God's victory. For, after almost two thousand years, where do we see the victory of the almighty God?

That victory will come when the earth will be radiant, when sin will really die out and have no more power, when Jesus will be king and the peoples of this earth become truly free in him. An out-and-out victory will not come until the kingdom of heaven itself is upon the earth. Our communities do a great deal; silent prayer in one's room is also of great value, but we are still waiting for the kingdom of heaven—a new revelation, a new unfolding of God's glory that is above everything we have known up to now.

This kingdom will at last come when the King himself makes his appearance. Yes, over the centuries we have had an inkling of this kingdom. Our faith has been prepared for it. But in the end, the kingdom of heaven will be like the ten virgins longing for the bridegroom to come. Our sole longing must be for the King to come. People already know they need this King. They know they are like sheep without a shepherd. They hunger and thirst for a king, although they rarely admit it. In response to this longing, we have to gather up all our strength in order to put ourselves under the Lord Jesus through our love. We must not seek our own interests anymore, but seek who Jesus is.

Only the wise virgins will be granted a part in the final gathering around the King, when further happenings will be talked over. No one who seeks his own interests can take part in these innermost talks with Jesus.

<hr>

The early Christians were looking forward to the second coming of Jesus. This proves that they knew something was not yet finished. They understood that Jesus had started something new, but that it awaited perfection. How Jesus will return remains hidden—it will most likely be quite different from the way we are used to picturing it. Among the early Christians, when believers were groaning under terrible oppression, in really bad times, they had all kinds of mystical, fanatical, millenarian ideas of Christ's second coming. Since then the picture of Christ's return has continued in the same colors, so to speak. But today we have to forgo our visions of how this will all work out. We must give God the freedom to act as he wills, for unknown to us, the kingdom of God can come and unfold in quite a simple, natural way.

↢

According to Scripture, it appears that Christ's return will be catastrophic. But we have to be very cautious here. In apostolic times they had no conception that things could really change, and so they could not imagine the future of Jesus Christ coming in any other way than through a huge collapse. They believed that when the Savior came there would be crashing and shaking in heaven, on earth, and under the earth. For them it was a question of keeping their hope alive against all odds, like a burning lamp, clearly visible. And because no one could imagine how God's kingdom could develop gradually, they pictured their hope as arriving like a shot from a gun: "Jesus is coming soon and will shatter the entire world!"

But to their descriptions we have to add the experience we have gathered since then. For instance, it took three hundred years to get no further than the collapse of the Roman Empire—God was also speaking through that experience. Then many other nations had to come under review, for God was searching, as it were, all around the globe for a people who might serve him faithfully. In the end, completely different nations were given a turn. By this we see how gentle God is. He seeks and seeks, until he finds something that can go forward. Consider, too, how slowly the relationship between Christianity and world events has developed. Only now has it gradually got so far that the Spirit of Jesus Christ can begin to work among the nations. God has time. God is always patient. With God it is never too late.

My father also had a "confession of hope": he hoped for a new outpouring of the Holy Spirit. And in his time, like with the early Christians, everyone assumed that such an outpouring, such a change would come about only through a catastrophe. He therefore imagined the Holy Spirit suddenly descending. Outwardly, however, things have worked out differently. Still he was right. Today his hope is being fulfilled, for we find that the Holy Spirit is coming, even though it goes unnoticed by the people. What is new is like a grain of seed in the world and grows in quiet. Only the "wise virgins" are aware that Christ is approaching. The reign of Jesus

Christ can be here before you notice it. One of these days, people will realize that something new has come, but they won't know where it came from.

✧

World history, human history, the history of the nations must come into Jesus' hands. It must come under his control so that people can no longer do just as they please.

✧

The Gospels describe the Savior's return as the arrival of the "Son of Man" in his glory. What extraordinary kindness is shown here! God will not overwhelm us, so to speak, with a glory that we can't bear. He will come in the glory of humankind, that is in the fullness of life and with the integrity that is intended for every person and that all people can understand. And because he comes in such a human way, he will appear "to all nations." Any person who is a true human being has significance for all humankind. Class distinctions and national differences disappear. That is why Jesus came "into the flesh." His future coming will again take place in the flesh, and when this happens he will be the Son of Man for all of humankind. He will take such control of our earthly circumstances that he can no longer be ignored.

✧

When the Son of Man appears he will come with eternal fire. Thank God! Those who align themselves with Satan will no longer be permitted to corrupt those around them. Eternal fire and the justice that comes with it will destroy the satanic fetters that bind humankind wherein people call what is bad, "good," and what is good, "bad."

Every person will be judged on the basis of whether his heart has been turned toward his fellow human beings or not. He will not be asked, "What did you believe, and what did you not believe?" All who show compassion can be of service in God's kingdom. Only those who are inhuman cannot be used. A person with heart may not yet understand Jesus, but this doesn't mean he despises Jesus or cannot be used by God. Many an unbeliever will enter the kingdom of heaven simply because his heart responds to the needs of others.

A person's humanity is demonstrated by the compassion he shows toward those whom the Savior calls "the least of these brothers and sisters of mine"—the weather-beaten and repulsive looking—and by his desire to free them from their prisons. The worst prison is often built by human society: anyone who is ostracized and rejected belongs to the Lord's poorest. Perhaps he is disagreeable, unsociable, and downtrodden. Maybe he is in despair or on the verge of mental breakdown. Perhaps he is a poor wretch and despised on account of being severely crippled. So he sits around, unable to work like other people. Yet when he dies, people say to themselves in astonishment, "What treasure we had in that man!" They then realize that he was one of the least of the Lord's brethren. Your treatment of these poorest of the poor will show whether you have any humanity in you or not. And for Jesus, the people's king, this is all that counts.

Those who are inhuman will have to get out. Often there are not many who need to be removed. Even so, a few individuals with satanic ideas can corrupt thousands. How good-natured and obedient people could be if certain heartless individuals were not among them. Many a village would soon come to rights if only two or three people were no longer there.

But judgment over the heartless can start today, in all quietness. This judgment is the beginning of God's kingdom, not the final end. However, one day whole nations will come out of the mire, and what is unclean will be separated from among them. Not until then will true civilization begin. The earth shall belong to the Lord. Things shall be set right with the earth and with the people on earth. That is the future of Jesus Christ, the Son of Man.

Judgment begins the moment when each person sees with his own eyes what he has done, when he sees himself for what he is, and when each person who is on the wrong track is brought to a halt. Such judgment is a blessing. You will not be blessed without such judgment. We must want judgment for ourselves and for all people, so that we are revealed as we really are.

There is no forgiveness without judgment. Everything brings its due reward. People need to feel that something is wrong before it can be set right. Otherwise it will not be corrected. Forgiveness simply means correction. If we have committed an offense, it must be atoned for, and then comes forgiveness. You must not bandage a wound if there is still dirt in it.

⌀

Jesus came to take away our sins (1 John 3:5). How he does this cannot be explained theologically. We can only believe it and put it into practice.

If sin is something that can be taken away, it means we human beings are more than our sin. When a tree is full of caterpillars, you can say that it is infested with caterpillars, but not that it is a caterpillar. You can take away the caterpillars. When we sin, we are sinful, but we are not our sin. We believe that we are creatures who can be cleansed from sin by the hand of God. In the course of time Jesus takes away the sins of all people, like foam.

To believe that Jesus Christ came to take away the sins of the world but then to say, "He cannot forgive my sin," is itself a sin. As people who believe in Christ we have to represent the truth to the world. We must, of course, first of all be ashamed of our sins. There has to be a break between us and worldly sins. We must cast off from ourselves the filth that is prevalent in the world. But then we need to turn ourselves toward our neighbor and together become staunch fighters on their behalf, knowing that Jesus came into the world to take sins away. Every misgiving, such as, "Perhaps I will be lost after all, or perhaps that person over there will be lost," makes room for the enemy to come in again. All anxiety increases the power of sin.

Our calling is to fight in faith for the Day of Jesus Christ, who takes away sin. Too many Christians are spurred by wrath, saying: "O that fire from heaven would fall upon this godless world!" Others strive to make this a better world but do so without any faith—they grow weary and fainthearted and eventually give up the struggle. Others blithely bear with equanimity the idea that millions will indeed have to perish in death and hell, while they themselves go to heaven. But none of these are true fighters. The Day of Christ will never come in these ways. If I open the door halfway and assert, "It isn't possible for God to take away everyone's sins," the serpent has won, and millions are plunged into darkness. A divided Jesus is not Jesus! If our faith in the Savior is weak we shall never see victory.

So let us make sure that in ourselves we have nothing more to do with sin. As for others, well, millions may indeed be cast into the fire, but only to the point where they feel ashamed and their sins can be taken away. God's judgment is severe, but he always judges with a view to salvation. Everything God does works for redemption.

⊶

In a human court of justice the judge determines the sentence. In divine jurisdiction, however, the guilty one passes judgment. God is silent. What happens is that the convicted becomes glad, saying, "Thank God, I have learned my lesson!" He joyfully submits to the mighty hand of God. This judgment is something one learns from; it is an education.

And so it is with the last judgment, where God intends to save human society. The human condition is such that we are still completely in the dark. Individuals here and there may be saved, but our society is not ready. Our human society gives rise to murder, adultery, fornication, theft, false witness, slander. Unless we are watchful day and night, we cannot escape society's influence. Light from above still has to come into our social life through judgment. And this light is starting to break in. Unlike in the past, nowadays people are asking different, more hopeful questions. We no longer ask, "How shall we start a war?" but, "How shall we make peace?" Not, "How shall we conquer a nation?" but, "How can others enjoy the opportunity for progress?" That these questions are in the air is a sign that we are coming closer to the last judgment. God's final judgment brings salvation to the nations of the earth.

⊶

When God finally judges the prince of this world, we shall not escape unscathed. The fire of judgment will shower sparks on us, too. Anyone who has done well for himself under the prince of this world will have to suffer great distress. But in the midst of his grief he will realize, "This is my good fortune."

People get torn to pieces whenever false human sovereignties collapse. They protest and in despair burst into tears. But, thank God, at last they weep!

Even in the midst of judgment we belong to God. So we can even help out, as long as we continue to believe that God is our Father. "You are our Father, God. Therefore, may your judgment arise and save us from all alien influences. For we belong to you, O God."

✧

In the end, there is nothing and no one in the world but God. Therefore, to declare the existence of a hell where for all eternity God has nothing more to say is nothing less than denying the gospel.

✧

Those who refuse to believe will be damned—which means, actually, that they will remain in the hell they are in already. Damnation is the end result of sin; it comes of its own accord. We are damned if we do not believe. The way of the world takes its course, and thus the fate of the world is our fate, too. So what are we to do? Believe! Let us direct all our energy to reverse the reality of damnation. See to it that you believe, and thus rid the world of damnation.

✧

We must fight to our last breath, to our last drop of blood that heaven and earth and the world of the dead come into the hands of Jesus. If I have to give up hope for one person, for one place, then the burden of death, the weight of woe, the oppression of night and darkness still remains, and then Jesus cannot come as the light of the world.

✧

The Bible says, "Behold, I make all things new" (Rev 21:5). People everywhere long and yearn for this. Christian faith has strengthened a longing in people for improvement; it sets them thinking that their lives have to change. But the Savior kindles a fire on earth, and to this belongs the yearning for everything to become new. Everything new! If the least bit of venom comes into our soul, everything is ruined right away. The least trace of evil results in a senseless waste of effort. Therefore, everything new: without exception, everything!

We must go whole hog with our hope and not let ourselves be disturbed by Bible texts we do not fully understand. Where God's words in Scripture strike home, they include everything, heaven and earth, in their promise. We human beings are so easily frightened, and in our intimidation we feel again and again half-damned. All the more we must embrace God's whole will: heaven new, earth new, a dwelling place of God right in our midst. God will wipe away all tears from our eyes.

Yes, the Bible says that the despairing, the unbelievers, the murderers, the immoral are all damned. We mustn't take this contradiction away from the Bible—it is simply there. But it won't do to preach about reconciliation and resurrection and then damn the people afterward. After all, isn't the soul of every person groaning? If we look at the whole of humankind, who can condemn? God is here. It is he who puts everything right.

Personally, I cannot affirm, "Heaven and hell. Both light and darkness. The devil and God." That is a divided world. This division holds true only for the time of struggle. In the end, only God counts, *only God*. So even if I am still to be punished at the end, in God's hands punishment is a blessing. With God, all dualism has to come to an end. And should it take thousands of years—there must still come wholeness. All things will be reconciled (Col 1:19–20). "Behold, I make all things new."

Striving for this is certainly not easy. To begin with, everything in us must become new. In other words, we have to hand over our lives. We have to go into the repair shop, so to speak, where *everything* in us has to be taken apart like an old machine. This naturally arouses fear and trepidation. But when we realize that Christ wants to make all things new, including us, then we receive strength to offer our lives to God and place ourselves on the altar. Such a sacrifice is a joy.

Jesus says he will make "everything new." Therefore, we must also sacrifice what is good—all that seems right to us and what we have grown accustomed to. Admirable traditions, pleasant company, one's nation, family, church—everything has to go into the repair shop. We have to surrender everything over to God, joyfully, completely, every day, in all circumstances. As long as we keep back areas of our life, saying, "That's something good," we will not become new. Everything must be given over to God. And when at last the whole will of God—his good, perfect, gracious will—is in our hearts, once God's whole will on earth corresponds to his whole will in heaven, then the greatest things can happen.

Will the Son of Man find faith on the earth when he comes? Will he find people who help him, who are totally ready for him? Or will he find people preoccupied with other things? There will be but a few who have given themselves over to his will. But even if there are only a few, the words will be fulfilled: "Behold, I make all things new!" One of these days, the bride of Jesus Christ will be ready, everything in the church will have reached the level it should, and then at last the advance of God's kingdom will take place quickly. But it will take time before this point is reached.

⊷

"The night is over; the day is here." It does not look at present as if it were day. Our feet still walk in sin; our hands do not manage to do anything good, genuine, or right. Around us there are thousands and thousands of people who are submerged in the mire of corruption. They die in masses. There appears to be no day on the earth. But our faith demands it, our love to God, our hope in God demands it, that we proclaim: "Nevertheless, the night is over, the day is here." The hour Jesus was born the day appeared. We have to say in the name of Jesus Christ, "It must become true on earth now, too! Jesus is Lord. So day must come."

What is this day? This day is God's love. It is day in your heart the moment you believe in God's love and remain in his love. The love of God melts away everything that is bad; everything that is sordid; everything that leads to despair. Love banishes the night and vanquishes death. But this love is not human love as we understand it. It is a godlike love that loves enemies; a love that rejects no one and nothing; a love that strides unswerving through everything, like a hero, and will not be insulted, despised, or rejected; a love that marches through the world with the helmet of hope on its head.

We simply are not bold enough to proclaim this love that Jesus is born and therefore all created beings are loved. We lack courage because we see so many people who seem to follow only their selfish desires—as if they enjoyed being sinners. But don't be fooled. No one enjoys being a sinner. Everyone groans under the weight of their sin. Every dying person sighs. God's love strides boldly in and among sinners—all who are groaning in death. God's love, which became fully human in Jesus Christ, is poured out into our hearts. Jesus wants all people to know that he himself is the boundless love of God. He is the flame by which we are purified to love. It is love alone, God's great compassion, which receives us into his judgment, so that we might become free from everything that enslaves us and makes us unhappy.

Because God is love, everything has to be loved. That is our business. We are children of the Father who loves us all. You then must love the Father in heaven, even if you do not understand. Somewhere deep inside you, you know the word "father"; at this everyone's heart must break, everyone's heart must love.

Let us thank the Father in heaven that Jesus is born—the day has come. We can let this day—already at hand—be manifested in our lives. We can fight for resurrection and life. Let everyone who is in any kind of trouble, fear, distress, or pain give thanks in spite of this. In giving thanks, your heart will grow light and you will become a co-fighter for God's love to pierce through the darkness and bring on the day.

And so we pray, not only for ourselves but for our brothers and sisters, too. Our hope is filled with love for all people. Throughout the world it is possible for us to become one church under God's reign. Though scattered we are united in one Spirit to believe, give thanks, and pray:

> Father in heaven, we praise you. You are great and mighty. You have straightened out everything in heaven and on earth and under the earth. You have called us to go into the darkest places with your love, to embrace our enemies with your love. You have called us to have the faith that permeates the world with love, until it is illuminated and shines in the light of your truth and justice—until everything is at peace and everything has been called from death into life. You hear the groans, and we hear them, too. You have given your Son for those who groan. And so we ask in your love, "Have mercy soon upon all of groaning creation. Have pity on all the creatures you have made. Surely you are compassionate. The night is over; the day is here!"
>
> Therefore, O Lord, we look forward with exultation to your kingdom in which you will crown Jesus Christ Lord. He will have the victory not only in heaven but on earth. The world will be righteous and we will be good to each other. We will find peace, and everything that happens will be according to your will. For the day shall certainly come when your will shall be done *everywhere* on earth, just as it is in heaven. Be with us with your Spirit so that we may stand steadfast as your children until the moment when we

can rejoice and say, "Come out from all affliction! Come out from all evil and all death! Come out to your Father in heaven." Praise be to you today. All glory to your kingdom! All glory be to Christ, our Savior, whom you have given to us and to the whole world. Amen.

# Introduction to the 1922 German Edition

*by Eugen Jäckh*

THE GOOD NEWS OF Jesus Christ is making its way through all nations. As it spreads, these words of God, once given as a promise are fulfilled: "Those who hope in the Lord will renew their strength. They will soar with wings like eagles" (Isa 40:31).

In some way, the gospel of Jesus Christ seems to be going out of fashion. It seems to be disappearing under the ruins of the ages. But time and again this good news rises up by the eternal power of God that it carries within it. It raises up people in whom the gospel of Jesus Christ comes to life and goes out into the world as the message of the living God.

In the Middle Ages individuals arose who, to the best of their understanding, strove to be nothing but disciples of Jesus Christ. In the Reformation the gospel was revealed again as the power of God that saves all those who believe in it. In spite of persecution, in spite of any false representation of the gospel, it continues to live, because behind it stands the Lord— Christ, the risen one. In his strength it goes forward from one renewal to the next, from resurrection to resurrection. It came into the world as the great message of salvation: "The time has come. The kingdom of God has come near" (Mark 1:15).

The gospel cannot rest until God's kingdom is fulfilled in heaven *and* on earth. And so it is coming back to life in our time with its world-embracing, world-changing power to create the future.

Eighty years ago (1842) in Württemberg, in a little village at the edge of the Black Forest, a new witness to this gospel appeared, not by his own strength and wisdom, but called through God's mighty deeds. Johann Christoph Blumhardt, in his small parish of Möttlingen, was led by the strong hand of God into conflict with dark powers; and not through any effort of his own. This occurred in connection with the illness of a girl in his congregation. During this struggle he turned to the living Savior as his only recourse, and he experienced the deep-going victory of Jesus Christ. "Jesus is Victor" was once again proclaimed—the gospel came to life again. It was not Blumhardt's faith or his personal ability that was victorious—only Jesus Christ himself. Jesus became the victor over all powers that oppress men and women.

A great movement began, comparable to the one that drove the people to John the Baptist in the desert. From the entire neighborhood, even from distant countries, people came who were troubled and tormented and they found help for body and soul. Forgiveness of sins became a power once more, and combined with that, diseases were healed—they simply fell away—so that people felt like they were back in Old Testament times.

But, since it was the good news of Jesus Christ that people were experiencing, Blumhardt could not rest on these achievements, for the gospel urges people forward to meet the coming Lord. The experiences that were granted to Blumhardt were simply a promise of a still more glorious future. The old prophecies in the Bible came alive, and people lifted up their heads, for redemption was drawing near. Their gaze was directed longingly to a new outpouring of the Holy Spirit upon all flesh. They yearned for the Lord to come, as promised, in power and majesty.

Blumhardt continued in this hope when he transferred his work from Möttlingen to Bad Boll. Thousands visited Bad Boll to quench their thirsting souls with the water of the living gospel. For them, too, the gospel proved to be the power by which God saved and healed.

Even the death of this man of God could not suppress the newly awakened hope. After he died, the same good news he proclaimed found a new voice in his son Christoph.

Christoph Blumhardt was born at Möttlingen on June 1, 1842, in the period when the fight against dark powers was most severe. His childhood coincided with the great victory of Jesus Christ, which was deeply and indelibly imprinted upon the child's soul. In Bad Boll the young man found himself in the midst of the stream of people seeking help, coming from all classes and countries. He naturally became a part of his father's ongoing struggle for the kingdom of God and chose the clerical profession. He served as a vicar in the Baden and Württemberg church and began supporting his father as his assistant. As his father lay dying, he laid his hands upon his son and said, "I bless you for the victory."

Christoph Blumhardt took up his father's work with deep humility. God's hand took hold of him, and he obeyed without any ulterior motives—only for the sake of the cause, a service that begged to be continued. His characteristic realism was immediately apparent from the way he succeeded his father: his life was always rooted in an objective attitude. As early as the 1880s he said,

> God's kingdom goes forward when we have an upright heart and when an angel comes close to us, grabs hold of us, and sets us down here or there, so that a whole network of God's answers to prayer is drawn around us, and we are so tightly bound up in it that we can hardly breathe. God's kingdom goes forward even when judgment and punishment fall on us, so that we can't get away with anything anymore, so that we have to renounce and surrender ourselves, so that we no longer climb up in our human strength but are shoved into the divine.

In an exegesis of the prophet Jeremiah, Blumhardt says, "The higher the divine, the more humbly it makes its appearance, as if it had to apologize to everyone." In great religious personalities the human aspect is of minor importance; the divine is what counts: "In the future we don't need to know what kind of person someone was or is. Nor is the main thing that we have a relationship with the Savior, but that the Savior has a relationship with us." The Spirit of God "is not an inherent strength, but a living, personal presence that can come to us or leave us."

It was this objective attitude that made it possible for Christoph Blumhardt to receive the same Spirit that worked so powerfully through his father. For years he experienced a torrent of divine miracles that healed many people in both soul and body—ample evidence that such power was not the human strength of a unique personality but the direct working of God and Jesus Christ. Like for his father, the gospel was alive.

But this same gospel also directed the son along ways different from those of his father. On earth there is a great danger that something alive becomes stiff or frozen. To treat what is holy in a superficial way is a similarly numbing process. As it happened in the days of Jesus Christ, it also happened in Bad Boll. The "miracles" people were experiencing became the "main" thing. Miracles in God's kingdom, however, have their meaning and justification only as "evidence" of something greater, as outward indications of the existence of an inner reality. If they are no longer understood this way, they should rather *stop*.

God let them subside, and Blumhardt clearly recognized this as God's will. This brought his pastoral activity all the more strongly to the fore, thus leading him to take on the care of innumerable wretched and burdened people. He was still surrounded by miraculous deeds of God, but they continued in holy quietness. Like a priest, Blumhardt carried not only the pleas for help of individual people, but through these requests he came face to face with the misery and poverty of all Christendom, yes, of the whole world.

Once more the gospel message came alive. God loved the whole world when he gave his only begotten Son. Christoph Blumhardt experienced the sad fact that all too often the most devout Christians have no concern for the needs of the world. They are content with a piety that assures them of their own salvation, while resigning themselves to the prospect of a world consigned to damnation. Blumhardt felt the direct opposite. His whole heart was open to the wretchedness and sin of the godless world and to the Father in heaven, who loves each and every person like a lost son and does not rest until he or she lies reconciled in his arms.

Is this God supposed to be at work only in the church? Shouldn't world events be under his guidance? Shouldn't discoveries of natural science be seen as revelations of God? Shouldn't inventions that benefit people's lives and the commerce of the nations also be seen as gifts from his hand? In this way, Christoph Blumhardt went further than his father. He combined his father's concepts of hope with the ideas of change and progress in our time. This enabled him to discover footprints of the living God and signs of the coming Savior in the events of the everyday.

This significant change in Blumhardt took place mainly in the last years of the nineteenth century. Most of the extracts compiled in this book are thus selected from the years 1896–1899. It was during this period where he proclaimed, with new language, the good news of God's love for the world.

It is not surprising that just at this period people from everywhere streamed to Bad Boll. Blumhardt was the center of interest in the house—a great, outstanding personality, a living witness to God, equipped with the power of the Spirit, with an inexhaustible wealth of ideas, and with vigorous speech. However, he came close to each person as pastor and spiritual adviser. He helped countless people in their troubles, from the highest classes to the simplest and poorest. He helped many who had lost courage to go on living; he strengthened the weak, comforted those who were sad, freed those who were bound, helped those nearing breakdown to get back on their feet, set right those who were confused, lifted up those who labored and were heavy laden—he preached the good news to the poor in personal, direct ways. This was because the good news of Jesus Christ was alive in him.

It has been said that saints are people in whose presence we are closer to God than at other times. We felt this with Christoph Blumhardt. In his presence one felt near to God. Something from above went out from him, which influenced his entire household and those he met.

The gospel also impelled him to go out into the world. Whereas the church had little hope for the world, the great social movement of our day inscribed its banners with new hope. If according to the belief of the prophets, even pagan peoples like the Assyrians, Babylonians, and Persians, and heathen kings like Nebuchadnezzar and Cyrus are in God's service, why shouldn't a socialist movement, for example, whose aim is to help humanity, also be an instrument in God's hand? Even though such a movement is too materialistic and temporal in its concerns—notions that have trickled down from the higher classes to the lower ones—nevertheless there is hidden in it a great deal of idealism and the nature of the Savior. For Blumhardt, a servant of Jesus Christ can join forces with whatever is in a movement that is allied to the Spirit of his Lord.

Blumhardt, however, was never a politician in the real sense of the word. He never wanted to be a party member, and only outer circumstances forced him into formally joining the Social Democratic Party. The people received him with open arms and hearts. In the long run, however, neither in political meetings nor in parliament, did he find the ground on which his witness to the gospel had full scope. After six years in politics he interpreted a long, serious illness to be a sign from God that he should return to the peace of Bad Boll.

Even here he kept his concern for and connection with the outside world. Just as before, all kinds of people came to his house, and he took part in their worries and aspirations, their work and their troubles and joys. His own task, however, was to proclaim the good news of the future kingdom of God and to watch and pray constantly. His "soul travailed" (Isa 53:11) day and night. The more clearly his eyes were illuminated by the light of Jesus Christ, the more clearly he saw the responsibility of a servant of God to represent the total forgiveness of sins to a world still covered in darkness. In this forgiveness—found through Jesus Christ—nothing is excluded and everything is reconciled. He saw in Christ the power that overcomes sin and creates a new world. This forgiveness brings about an atmosphere in which a new revelation of the risen one can bring God's kingdom where justice and peace dwell. "God's kingdom is God's objective. It shapes history and leads us to an experience of God—until the coming Day dawns."

The gospel is the good news of this future Day of Jesus Christ. "The Savior is coming!" This promise runs like a bright thread through all Blumhardt's thinking.

Did the Savior actually come to him? Did the eyes of this Simeon see the Savior?

Eventually Blumhardt quietly and meekly had to accept the decline of his physical strength, which resulted from a stroke. He departed from this life in deep peace on August 2, 1919. Before he was taken ill, the time of the World War and world revolutions had set in. Some might ask, "Where is your God now?" We "looked for good to rule, but saw bloodshed; for justice to prevail, but saw justice perverted!" (Isa 5:7). Our day seems to have brought us just the opposite of what men like Johann Christoph Blumhardt and his son hoped for.

But seen truly, what they experienced was the beginning of the fulfillment of God's promise. As has been said, prophets precede great events as storm petrels precede the storm. These men of God were heralds of coming events. Let us thank God that there were prophets of salvation to precede the disasters of our day, as Hosea, the prophet of love, preceded the destruction of the kingdom of Israel, and Isaiah and Jeremiah, the heralds of the Messiah and the new covenant, preceded the destruction of Judah.

The clouds continue piling up and darkening the earth; the final battle between light and darkness has begun. How often in Bad Boll did we sing: "The old world is collapsing, and the kingdom of Jesus Christ alone arises on its ruins." The old world is collapsing. It has to fall, so that the new world can be established. And the great battle of which we are witnesses is simply the final tremendous battle, which will be won by Jesus, the victor. That is why the father Blumhardt could die with the parting words, "The Lord will open his mild hand in mercy over all nations." And that is why the son Blumhardt during his last days of suffering and death could cling like a child to the assurance: "The Savior is coming!"

Two witnesses of the gospel are gone. But because they were witnesses of the good news of Jesus Christ, they continue to live. The gospel always lives, and whoever has witnessed for the gospel lives with it. There will always be an interest in the Blumhardts, both father and son. But of much greater significance is the resurrection of the gospel. In our day, the gospel is coming alive again. Many eyes are watching for Jesus Christ. In the one "who was there," more and more people see the one "who is coming."

No sect, no church, no movement is attached to the name of Blumhardt. But without any evident connections, the thoughts of these two prophets are stirring here and there in the world today. For the Lord is Spirit and creates buds and blossoms wherever he will. He has his cause in hand. He keeps his gospel alive from resurrection to resurrection until it is fulfilled in his time.

At Epiphany 1922

# Scripture Index

## OLD TESTAMENT

### Genesis

| | |
|---|---|
| 2:17 | 37 |
| 22:18 | 90 |

### 1 Samuel

| | |
|---|---|
| 2:1–10 | 90 |

### Isaiah

| | |
|---|---|
| 5:7 | 124 |
| 9:2 | 12 |
| 24:23 | 16 |
| 40:31 | 59, 119 |
| 42:2 | 34 |
| 42:3 | 86 |
| 42:6–7 | 34 |
| 43:2 | 61 |
| 49:4 | 59 |
| 49:8 | 59 |
| 53:11 | 123 |
| 60:1 | 58 |

### Daniel

| | |
|---|---|
| 9 | 82 |

## NEW TESTAMENT

### Matthew

| | |
|---|---|
| 5:3 | 68 |
| 5:6 | 71 |
| 5:43 | 93 |
| 5:44–48 | 93 |
| 8:8 | 89 |
| 10:32 | 55 |
| 11:30 | 78 |
| 16:24 | 84 |
| 24:13 | 102 |
| 24:42 | 53 |
| 27:46 | 68 |
| 28:18 | 53 |
| 28:19–20 | 54 |
| 28:20 | 76 |

### Mark

| | |
|---|---|
| 1:15 | 119 |
| 7:34 | 44 |
| 16:15 | 76 |

### Luke

| | |
|---|---|
| 1:46–55 | 90 |
| 2:34 | 22 |
| 6:20 | 68 |
| 6:24 | 68 |

## Luke (*continued*)

| | |
|---|---|
| 9:22 | 39 |
| 12:16–21 | 68 |
| 14:27 | 78 |

## John

| | |
|---|---|
| 3:16 | 81 |
| 5:53 | 57 |
| 7:51–56 | 57 |
| 8:23 | 55 |
| 8:44 | 81 |
| 10:8 | 84 |
| 14:12 | 24 |

## Acts

| | |
|---|---|
| 1:3 | 20 |
| 2:23 | 52 |

## Romans

| | |
|---|---|
| 8:25 | 98 |
| 8:35 | 1 |

## 1 Corinthians

| | |
|---|---|
| 12:2 | 64 |
| 16:14 | 91 |

## 2 Corinthians

| | |
|---|---|
| 5:17 | 33 |

## Galatians

| | |
|---|---|
| 2:20 | 41 |

## Ephesians

| | |
|---|---|
| 1:7 | 36 |
| 6:12 | 94 |

## Philippians

| | |
|---|---|
| 2:6 | 84 |

## Colossians

| | |
|---|---|
| 1:19–20 | 115 |
| 3:10 | 33 |
| 3:11 | 41 |

## Hebrews

| | |
|---|---|
| 10:31 | 12 |

## 1 Peter

| | |
|---|---|
| 2:9 | 66 |
| 2:24 | 79 |
| 4:7 | 103 |

## 2 Peter

| | |
|---|---|
| 1:19 | 23 |
| 3:10 | 94 |
| 3:12 | 94 |

## 1 John

| | |
|---|---|
| 2:6 | 56 |
| 3:5 | 112 |
| 4:3 | 29 |

## Revelation

| | |
|---|---|
| 1:7 | 80 |
| 14:6 | 106, 107 |
| 14:7–8 | 107 |
| 21:5 | 43, 114 |

# The Blumhardt Source Series

## Johann Christoph Blumhardt
*A Biography*
Friedrich Zündel

## The Gospel of God's Reign
*Living for the Kingdom of God*
Christoph Friedrich Blumhardt

## Gospel Sermons
*On Faith, the Holy Spirit, and the Coming Kingdom*
Johann Christoph Blumhardt

## Make Way for the Spirit
*My Father's Battle and Mine*
Christoph Friedrich Blumhardt

Lightning Source UK Ltd.
Milton Keynes UK
UKHW010823200819

348226UK00003B/51/P